Praise for Jane Morri

D0209067

"Ms. Morris is a brave genius for putting the truth out there and letting it fly. Bravo!"

Deanna Silverman,
Host of Hilarious Humanitarians Podcast

"Morris opens up about the comical misery that has become the teaching profession-giving a voice to teachers everywhere."

Parent Herald

"One of the funniest teacher books you'll ever read!"

Bored Teachers

"A well written, hilarious and accurate description of what teachers deal with in their classrooms every day. There is more to this book than just funny stories. There is a lot of commentary on the state of teaching today. Worth every penny."

Amazon

"Should be required reading for any college student or adult, especially those who are NOT teachers. Painfully true, hysterically accurate, Morris beautifully articulates what it means to be a teacher today. You will be horrified and entertained!"

Goodreads

"I dare you not to laugh out loud!"

Robin O'Bryant, New York Times bestselling
author of *Ketchup is a Vegetable and Other Lies Moms Tell Themselves*

"Jane is a gifted storyteller, you will chuckle and you will sigh. The perfect gift for your kid's teacher or a teacher friend!"

Joyce Kaufman, Ed.D,
Host of The Joyce Kaufman Show, Newstalk 850 WFTL

"Jane Morris gives us a beautifully written exposé about the worst sides of today's students, parents and school administrators."

Bruce Tulgan, bestselling author of
Not Everyone Gets a Trophy: How to Manage the Millennials

"Jane Morris lifts the curtain on the horror teachers in our country face every day."

Laurie Notaro, New York Times bestselling author of

"The stories Morris tells are unbelievable and yet, I'm positive they're true."
Jen Mann, New York Times bestselling author of
People I Want to Punch in the Throat

"Morris dishes on the truth about trying to teach in this culture and it is hilarious, informative, and insightful."
Stefanie Wilder Taylor, New York Times bestselling author of *Sippy Cups Are Not for Chardonnay*

"A compelling answer to anyone thoughtless enough to assert that teachers have it easy."
John Owens, author of *Confessions of a Bad Teacher*

"As funny as it is shocking."
LibraryThing

"This is one of the best books I've ever read!"
Kathryn Raaker, host of Let's Just Talk Radio, on Teacher Misery

"The stories that Morris tells about the school system are riveting. The antics and violence and outright stupidity that she and other teachers have had to endure are outright insane — some of it is so crazy it's almost unbelievable."
Mission Incomplete

"Let me be honest, nonfiction books are not my cup of tea, but this book is simply amazing, hilarious, and kept surprising me nonstop!"
Jessica's Book Blog

"This book is just the most hilarious and heartbreaking ever! Laugh out loud funny!"
Teachers Are Terrific

"Her stories are so ridiculous, that a non-educator might actually believe they're fabricated. Unfortunately, those of us who are on the inside know it's all too real. Her stories are laugh out loud funny, touching, and at times, maddening."
Having a Mom Moment

"This book is a great read and a real eye-opener."
Carpe Librum

"Morris is a great writer who did a great job presenting her case. She is funny and entertaining. She is above all honest with her interpretation of the things that she sees around her. I liked the variation in text and material. Overall, these books need to be spread around the country. She isn't the only person that feels this way. There are thousands of other people out there like her and their voices need to be heard."

The Next Book on my List

"This was a HILARIOUS read!"

The Simply Organized Teacher

"Filled with dry wit, Morris illuminates the lives of those to whom we owe a hell of a lot."

Luke Marlowe, The Page Is Printed

More Teacher Misery

Nutjob Teachers,
Torturous Training,
& Even More Bullshit

JANE MORRIS

FOR M,

Always for you.

Also by Jane Morris

Teacher Misery: Helicopter Parents, Special Snowflakes & Other Bullshit

Crap My Students Make

The Mystery of Existence & Love the Ones You're With:
2 Comedic Plays by the Author of Teacher Misery

CONTENTS

"This is an abomination of
catastrophic proportions."

*-Parent email to teacher, expressing her displeasure with her daughter receiving a zero
for not turning work in on time*

PREFACE

When I first started teaching over a decade ago, I immediately thought, "Yeah, there's no way I can do this." It was completely different from my experience as a student, and as an intern. My secondary education studies in no way prepared me for it. I thought, "Just make it through this year and you'll figure something out."

As that year got more and more challenging, I started to collect materials. I grabbed a folder and wrote, "No one will believe this bullshit" on it and started stuffing it full of absurd artifacts from all aspects of my job. If a kid sent a rude email, I printed it out and stuck it in the folder. If an administrator gave me a bullshit evaluation based on arbitrary things such as "blinds not pulled up evenly," I made a photocopy and in it went. I wasn't sure why I was documenting everything. I just knew that if I didn't, no one would believe what I was experiencing and it needed to be shared.

As the year continued, my experiences were so outrageously awful that even veteran teachers admitted that I got more shit in my first year than they had experienced in their whole careers. I started to think that I was a bullshit magnet, or just a really shitty teacher.

Now I know better.

Those teachers hadn't had all of those experiences because teaching didn't become as awful as it is now until recently. Now, when veteran teachers read my book, they recognize how much their chosen career has changed, and figure out how to retire early.

"Just make it through this year. You can't be the kind of person who quits in the middle of the year. You're stronger than that," I told myself. And then the same administrator who commented on my blinds, and later advised me to "treat kids like sacks of shit," invited me into her office. She offered the following wisdom: "You know, I just want to commend you. Most people in their first year of teaching who have experienced half of the difficult situations that you have would have quit by now. Honestly, I'm really surprised that you haven't quit yet!"

That changed something in me.

I always knew I would be a teacher. I almost couldn't escape it, though I tried. I had different majors in college, and refused to acknowledge what I knew to be true: teaching was in my blood. I couldn't let these fuckers break me. "You're surprised that I haven't quit yet? Well, keep watching!" I thought. "Not only am I going to stay, I'm going to get really good at this!"

So I stayed, and I *did* get really good at it. And I also got much tougher, took less shit, and learned one of the most important lessons there is for a teacher: If you can't fix it on your own, it ain't getting fixed, so learn to ignore it as much as you can. It's just another day, even when a kid threatens other students with a box cutter and receives no consequence. It's just another day, even when a student tells you to suck a dick. It's just another day.

If I were going to survive the bullshit and continue to endure, I would need an outlet or I would make myself sick. I started turning my folder of bullshit into a collection of short stories. It was extremely therapeutic and even fun. From the outside looking in, a lot of what had occurred in my teaching past was pretty funny. So I started making jokes about it on Instagram. I held nothing back. It felt *amazing*.

Every day, before and after school and before bed, I shared my experiences and frustrations. Without this outlet, I would never have lasted as long as I have. It turns out that my experiences were not as outrageous as I had thought. Thousands and thousands of people started to contact me to share their gratitude that someone was telling the truth. We're not supposed to talk about anything that goes on in our profession in a negative way. It's not "professional." Well, neither is putting the safety of students and teachers in jeopardy on a daily basis.

I honestly never thought I would write a sequel to *Teacher Misery*. I believed I had covered every shitty aspect of teaching in the first book. But then I realized that I really had only told *my* story. And not only is my story far from over, but there are many other stories to tell.

In *More Teacher Misery*, I tell more of *your* stories. I share the experiences that have been shared with me from across the country and from other parts of the world. As I said, teachers are expected to be professional at all times, even in the most unprofessional of settings. Society as a whole can treat us like complete trash. We are expected to take endless verbal and even physical abuse, all while maintaining a completely calm and professional demeanor. And if you're an elementary school teacher, you're expected to do it with a smile on your face as rainbows shoot from your ass.

Teachers are society's scapegoat. We are expected to not only teach each and every child, regardless of their limitations, but we are also required to be social workers, nurses, therapists, disciplinarians, activists, fundraisers, and substitute parents while providing students with supplies, food, and endless encouragement. We are expected to do all of this with pathetic pay and little to no respect. When something inevitably goes wrong, we are the first to get blamed.

Perhaps if the general public knew what the daily lives of American teachers are really like, they would have some sympathy, and maybe even a little respect. Maybe if people knew that there are no longer any consequences for even the most violent and inappropriate behaviors, they would respect the teaching profession a bit more. It could be that if the public understood that we are working against impossible odds, with minimal resources, they would find ways to help improve the system.

It's a pretty farfetched dream… but I'm willing to give it a fucking try.

NOTE

Everything in this book, with the exception of names and locations, is true as far as I know. This is a compilation of my own experiences and the experiences that thousands of other teachers have shared with me. All names have been changed, including my own, to protect identities.

In an effort to be hip, I will use faces from popular memes and emojis to express my reactions and emotions. (Though my students would tell you these haven't been cool since 2011.) Here is a general key:

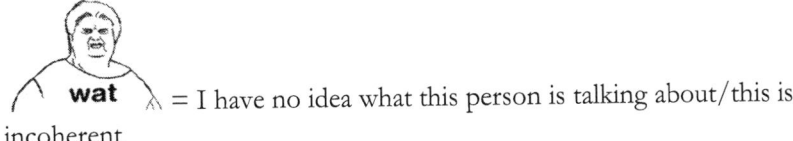 = I have no idea what this person is talking about/this is incoherent

 = As angry and frustrated as humanly possible

 = Are you fucking kidding me?

 = Sarcastic laugh

 = Well, excuse me!

 = Embarrassment and shame for someone else

 = Were you dropped on your head as a child?

 = What the fuck were you thinking?

 = Not bad

 = True story/universal truth

 = Jaded and judgmental

 = Please somebody help me

 = Fuck you

 = Fuck you, from a bear

 = I'm feeling like a circus monkey

1

HOW TO SPIN A PLATE AND OTHER THINGS I LEARNED AT PD

"Thank you teacher safety training,

for reminding me not to pick up vomit

with my bare hands."

Professional development is defined as "a variety of specialized training, formal education, or advanced professional learning intended to help teachers improve their professional knowledge, competence, skill, and effectiveness." I honestly don't think most teachers would have a problem going to these trainings if we actually learned something from them. Instead, they are almost always a torturous mixture of reiterating the same things we've heard dozens of times, embarrassing us, treating us like morons, and making us do mindless activities until we get so angry we feel like we are going to explode.

Allow me to give you an example (I'll be giving many actually, so grab a box of wine and get comfortable). A few years ago I had to attend a week-long, 40-hour training session in the summer. The title of the course was something like "Incorporating Literacy in the Secondary Classroom." I was confused by this because, as an English teacher, pretty much all I do is promote literacy. But I tried to keep an open mind before attending this week of cruel and unusual development. Honestly, after 40 hours spent in that class, I cannot for the life of me tell you what it was about, or what I was supposed to have learned. The class was taught by an elementary-level professional development specialist. So basically the woman who was going to teach middle and high school teachers how to teach was: 1) *not* a teacher, and 2) *never* worked in a secondary setting. Cool.

For someone who works with little kids, this lady did not have a lot of patience. She put what she called "manipulatives" on every table. She explained that these items had the potential to help students focus. It was basically a pile of toys on the table and soon after, in our desperate state of boredom, we began to play. This did not, in any way, make it easier for us to focus. While the teacher lectured us about… der… something, we were having a blast. There were lots of squishy things and we squished the shit out of them. We took the suction cup thingys and stuck them on each other. We threw the slimy stuff at the wall and marveled as it slowly slid to the floor. But the most engrossing activity, by far, was the playdough. Since the class was held in the cafeteria, we were able to find a lot of interesting objects to add to our playdough sculptures. My most admired creations were a lizard emerging from a woman's body and a queen made out of an old potato skin I found under the table. A neighbor fashioned some high heels out of silly putty for her. I guess our use of the manipulatives made it difficult for the teacher to focus because at one point she stomped over, snatched them all off the table and yelled, "They're not supposed to be used like that!"

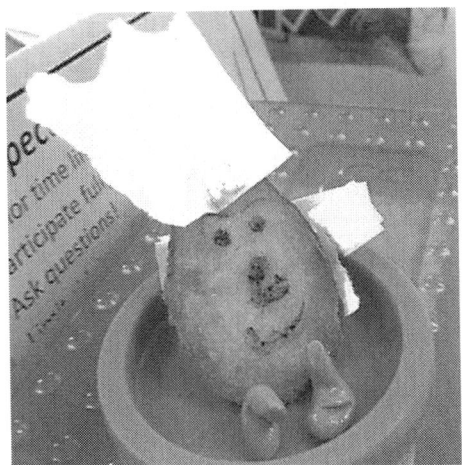

"Geez miss... I was just trying to focus better in your class!" I thought.

That was the first eight hours of this workshop. On the next day, things got really interesting.

We had to push all the tables to the perimeter of the room and form a big circle. Each person was given a piece of paper with the name of an animal written on it. We were instructed to listen to the teacher read a kindergarten level book about the rainforest, and every time we heard the name of our animal, we were supposed to make the corresponding noise as loud as we could. As much as I wanted to participate and "develop professionally," I had a big problem. The animal I was given was a "cock-of-the-rock." I didn't have a damn clue what that was. I asked everyone around me, and no one knew. Then I was told to "shhhhh!" So instead of asking for clarification I just waited in confusion until my animal was called. "And the cock-of-the-rock said...?" After a brief pause, I let out a noise that I felt was generic enough to fit most animals. It was like a high pitched "meeeeehhhh." The teacher looked at me with disdain and said, "What was that?"

"I don't really know because I have no idea what a cock-of-the-rock is!"

"It's a bird!" she yelled with condemnation. "Try again!"

Even though I now knew to make a bird noise, I wasn't sure what kind of bird noise to make. In a moment of sheer panic, I yelled, "Quack! Quack!"

Everyone was laughing their asses off except for the teacher.

"A *bird*! Not a *duck*!"

"Geez, for an elementary teacher you don't have much patience do you?" I thought. Then I remembered that she was not actually a teacher--and it all made sense.

"Cuck-caw!" I said, with less enthusiasm. "Was that a bird noise?"

With that, the "teacher" continued reading.

Soon after, a few teachers came out in various rainforest themed costumes and just stood there, looking humiliated. She then launched into a lecture about how to make literature come alive in the classroom.

I saw what she was going for, and I'm sure my 4-year-old would have loved it. The only problem was that every teacher there taught 7-12th grade. I think you'll agree that if you tried to make a teenager dress up as a bird, you would get punched in the face. I don't think any animal involving the word "cock" would go over well either.

The rest of the week we listened to her drone on and on about her kids, how much she hated her kids' teachers and other various (boring) musings on life. We also played games such as Bananagrams, Sock Wars and Hot Potato, all of which my daughter plays in preschool.

Forty hours of my life were lost to complete and utter bullshit.

And this is fairly common for most professional development workshops. Once in a while, they will start out in a helpful, relevant way, but they beat the same points into you so many times that when you hear a certain educational term, you react like someone with PTSD. Just say the word "differentiation" near a teacher and watch them shudder.

We have weekly training sessions and are often required to do some on the weekend and over the summer. A hot topic this year was "cultural competency." The National Education Association defines this as, "having an awareness of one's own cultural identity and views about difference, and the ability to learn and build on the varying cultural and community norms of students and their families." At my first cultural competency training, I was pleasantly surprised. The activities and discussions were actually interesting and relevant. We examined our own cultural beliefs and backgrounds and learned a lot about the beliefs of others. This 8 hour day probably could have been squeezed into 3 hours, but I was content with the fact that what we did was actually useful. The only problem was that this was a FORTY HOUR workshop.

The rest of the week was spent going over the same concept *ad nauseam*. By the end of the week, I was ready to bitch smack anyone who even mentioned the word "culture" or "bias." I made it through the week and went on living my life. But then our back to school two-week-long professional development started. And right there on the agenda were several 3-hour-long workshops about cultural competence. And in those workshops, we did *the exact same activities that we did during the summer*. It felt like a cruel joke. I was sure that at any moment the administrators were going to jump out from behind a curtain and proclaim, "Just kidding! We know you did this already! Now go and set up your classrooms! Make good use of your time!"

But I didn't really believe that because I know how things work. After we suffered through the pre-service weeks, we were called into the auditorium for our first staff meeting on the first day of school. And guess what the topic of discussion was! *How'd ya know?*

I felt like standing on the table and screaming, "There has to be another way! Please don't make us do the same graphic organizer or I might explode!" But instead, we just sat there, seething, because that's what we teachers do. We eat shit, and we pretend to like it.

Other mandatory professional development classes and what I learned from them:

Bloodborne Pathogens Training: I learned not to pick up vomit with my bare hands.

Incorporating Technology in the Secondary Classroom: I learned how to use Google.

Strategies for the Differentiated Classroom: I learned that if anyone asks, I should say that I differentiate everything.

Reading Strategies: I learned to follow along with my pointer finger when I read.

Solving Classroom Discipline Problems: I learned that bad behavior is *my* fault. My lessons are not exciting enough.

Gang Prevention Training: I learned that if a student is wearing a bandana, they are probably in a gang.

An Introduction to Peer Mediation: I learned that when kids try to kill each other, it is helpful to have them sit in a circle, possibly on a cheerful rug, and discuss their feelings.

Professional development courses tend to fall into five basic categories: mindfulness, safety, technology, team building and total bullshit (they're *all* bullshit, but these are particularly shitty and without purpose). I asked my teacher followers to describe their worst professional development experiences. Here is a rundown of the most interesting of the bunch:

Mindfulness and relaxation PDs:

"They made us do laughter yoga where the teachers stand in a circle and try to laugh in many different ways in front of their peers. The facilitator became upset that I kept sitting down (I was sick) so she moved my chair without me knowing. When I went to sit down again, I fell and struck my head on a table and got a concussion." *You should have sued! You could be on a beach in Hawaii sipping Mai Tais instead of going to the next ridiculous PD!*

"We had to do country line dancing to relieve stress." *Sounds pretty fucking relaxing!*

"An inspirational speaker preached to us about relaxation and meditation- -seemed promising until she started talking about how ineffective prescription medication is and that we should be treating depression and stress with 'other' techniques. Then she made us all do a massage train." *That sounds like a harassment lawsuit waiting to happen!*

"A woman spoke to us about stress management. She told us to get outside and take a walk during our 'lunch break.' She was shocked to find out we only get 25 minutes for lunch and have to use that time to go to the bathroom, make copies, and grade papers." *Isn't it fascinating how the people who try to teach teachers have no clue what teachers actually do all day long?*

"During a session about meditation and calming strategies in the classroom we were told to shut our eyes and relax our 'genitals.'" *I'll be sure to use that one with my students!*

"A professional came in to teach us 'mindfulness,' and we had to taste raisins and describe the way they felt on our tongues." *Are you trying to say that you don't find the taste of raisins relaxing???*

"We learned how to make a cupcake 'healthy.' " *Not sure what that has to do with education but I do enjoy cupcakes.*

Teaching methods PDs:

"In a training on behavioral problems we were told if we gave kids omega vitamins and fish oil it would solve all behavior problems." *If this is true, I am going to start giving out fruit punch spiked with fish oil. Desperate times call for weird, unproven and probably illegal measures.*

"I learned how *not* to be a 'worksheet teacher' by doing a bunch of worksheets." *Ah yes, the old "don't do what I'm doing and forcing you do" professional development strategy.*

"We did a 'snowball' fight where we all wrote down our most innovative ways of teaching the same standard, wadded the paper into balls, and threw them around the room while 'Let it Go' from Frozen played." *Makes sense to me! It's about expressing your frustration about the shitty forced standards, right?*

"We made a cell phone case out of pipe cleaners, cardboard, and fasteners and then sold it like an infomercial. No idea why." *Probably because you have to "sell the lesson plan" or some horseshit like that.*

"I sat in an hour-long PD to learn how to greet every student by name (and with a compliment) as they entered the classroom. The facilitator came back to make sure we were following through with it. Imagine a woman standing next to you with a clipboard watching you say hello to 33 students one by one, and writing down the compliments you gave." *I tried to imagine that but it took so long just picturing it that I fell asleep.*

"We spent half a day on making seating charts and the other half on how to give 'the look' to get kids to behave." *Hey, don't underestimate the power of THE LOOK. I'm a grown ass woman, and I still tremble when my mom whips that out!*

"During 'learning literacy strategies for 8th graders' it took us six 45-minute-long sessions to read and highlight the story of the three little pigs and determine the meaning of the story." *Ironic that the pigs represent the repressed desire to work less and the wolf is the powerful authority figure who drives you to work hard and do things you don't want to do out of fear. Sound familiar?*

Safety PDs:

"A guy came to our school to discuss school shootings and how to protect ourselves and the kids. He basically told us to throw a laptop at the gunman and leave the kids." *If it's your own personal laptop, it isn't worth the risk. If it's one of the school's shitty Chromebooks- go for it!*

"We had several ladder safety courses- some that lasted for hours with videos and demonstrations." *Considering all that ladder climbing that teachers do, this is actually pretty important!*

"The worst was the 'please stop going to the ER, it's costing the district too much money' PD." *Well is splitting your head open or breaking your wrist REALLY a good reason to waste the district's money? Don't be so selfish!*

"We had to attend a training on how to wash your hands correctly." *Before you knock it, are you sure everyone knows that you dry your hands AFTER you wash them?*

"We had an anti-bullying training which required us to take turns sitting in a circle while other teachers went around the circle saying mean things to us." *Don't underestimate the usefulness of feedback from colleagues!*

Technology PDs:

"We spent four hours learning to use an online assessment system. We didn't have Wi-Fi in our building, and we weren't getting Wi-Fi in our building." *Perhaps you might move to a wealthier district in the future that has access to Wi-Fi? They want to make sure you're prepared!*

"We had a four-hour training on how to send an email. They even brought in a Microsoft consultant." *Although most people would find that to be a useless training session, my mom would really appreciate it! (Sorry mom. Love you.)*

"They showed us some cool tech programs and then said we only get the free version which can't do shit." *Since teachers end up buying everything themselves, this was probably a big infomercial! I bet the district even got a cut!*

"They made us watch a presentation about how to get away from just using PowerPoint, by a guy who used PowerPoint to do his entire presentation." *And the level of boredom you experienced, along with the murderous feeling you felt, convinced you to avoid using PowerPoint I'm sure. Mission accomplished!*

Team building PDs:

"We had to participate in a drum circle." *And the problem is…?*

"We had to stand in a circle and all massage each other's shoulders to stress the importance of touch." *I guess your district has extra funds to handle a few harassment suits. Totally worth it!*

♪ "We had a full day conference in which we spent the first three hours doing a music 'workshop' where we built instruments out of garbage and then played a song for others to guess, whilst a 'lead teacher' from the district (who no longer worked in the classroom) came around and made patronizing comments." *I wouldn't want to do it but I would pay good money to watch!*

"We had to get into small groups and frost a pound cake. Some teams had pound cakes that were all cut up and some had whole cakes. The cakes were supposed to represent students." *Every child is like a special pound cake and every cake deserves to be frosted successfully. Also, free cake!!!!!*

"All the employees had to walk across the gym in a weird way that was different from everyone else. It was recorded and played at the next meeting." *Ah, the old "public humiliation caught on tape" PD! It's a classic!*

"We were forced as a full faculty to stand in a circle and do the nae nae." *Again, I wouldn't want to do it but I would pay good money to see it!*

"A juggler came and we had to juggle with our peers." *And the problem is…?*

"We did a game of faculty rock, paper, scissors to 'build school climate.'" *I would have gone with scissors every time to represent the violent school climate they were creating by making us play rock, paper, scissors.*

"We played a game called 'Touch Someone Who…'" *Sounds like the perfect opportunity to harass someone you've been meaning to harass for a while.*

"We were broken up into groups, taught a line dance, and then we had to perform the line dance in front of the other groups." *Yup. I wouldn't want to do it but I would pay a lot of money to see it!*

"We played musical chairs as an icebreaker for a department of grown ass adults who had known each other for years. We were already so comfortable with each other that people got bruised and body-blocked in the fight over chairs." *That actually sounds like fun. Stupid, pointless fun.*

Total bullshit PDs:

"We sat in a classroom with no air conditioning for three days in August while having the faculty handbook read to us word for word." *Sounds like a new reality show called Teacher Survivor.*

"I traveled three hours for PD on color coordinating classroom decorations." *Clashing colors can cause a lot of anxiety for some very fashion-conscious students. Where is your empathy?*

"Our principal printed out every single email she received from the school year, and we had to organize them into different piles under the guise of data review, personal emails included." *That sounds inappropriate, but I won't tell anyone, I swear!*

"They hired a street artist who prepared nothing prior to arriving in front of a room full of art teachers. He turned on R&B and gave us a private interpretive/exotic dance that involved pantomiming with a concrete pole." *I'd take that over a meeting about differentiation any day of the week!*

"We had a meeting about HOW TO HAVE A MEETING." *Well, are you sure everyone understands that have to keep your pants on the whole time? This is a critical element of having a successful meeting!*

"For hours, teachers seriously debated the pros and cons of keeping the door propped open, using a door stopper, or just opening and closing the door each time a student needed to exit the room." *Or you could do what I do which is lock that fucking door. I don't trust anyone these days!*

"During Advanced Placement Literature training we had to perform a Renaissance dance." *Again, I wouldn't want to do it but I would pay good money to see it!*

"For 3 hours we compared and contrasted success and achievement." *And I'm sure you all agreed that every student deserves both (even if they don't come to school or do any work)!*

"We got to take printed state testing data and rewrite it by hand." *I have no witty retort, only a giant middle finger.*

"We all had to drive in a car around the city on a scavenger hunt. If the principal wasn't in my car, I would have gone home." *This is why people drink and drive.*

"I had to spin a plate." *If it was a real plate, then that might be a great way to blow off steam!*

"We had to attend a session called 'How to blow a whistle correctly.'" *This is extremely useful for P.E. teachers! Think of all the whistleblowing they do in a day!*

"The district paid a woman thousands of dollars, twice, to explain her classroom management strategies. She told us to use old ties with Velcro to hold kids in their seats." *I would absolutely do that! And if anyone questioned me, I'd remind them that I learned that strategy in an expensive, mandatory professional development workshop!*

> I will not like to have this Job because want be a bartender because I want Make drinks for People. And I would Make My Self drinks too.

Me too, Kid. Me too.

2

DISGRUNTLED DEBBIE AND OTHER TEACHERS YOU'LL FIND IN ANY SCHOOL

"Okay, here's the deal. I have a hangover.

Who knows what that means?"

"Doesn't that mean you're drunk?"

"No. It means I was drunk YESTERDAY."

School of Rock

There are certain stereotypes about teachers that are absolutely true. Not all teachers embody these stereotypes, but I can guarantee that each school has one teacher who represents each one perfectly.

Miss Matchy-Matchy

This is usually a female teacher who color coordinates every inch of her body. If yellow is her chosen color for the day, not only will her dress and shoes be yellow, but her necklace, earrings and hair ornament will be yellow as well. She has a chunky necklace in every color. She is cheerful but to a weird, unnatural degree. She's probably got some pretty dark secrets that she's overcompensating for.

The Copy Machine Creature

This person has an unnatural obsession with the photocopy machine. She babysits the machine like it's her newborn child. She takes personal ownership over the copier and in her view, everyone is always fucking with her machine or about to break it. If the creature is in the copy room, expect to be yelled at.

John Keating

This is the young teacher who got into teaching to change lives! It isn't enough that he puts his mind, body, and soul into planning and implementing lessons. He also holds therapy sessions during lunch and after school. He is not just here to teach. He is here to inspire! And he will surely burn out before he gets tenure.

Disgruntled Debbie

This person is at her breaking point at all times! If you want to complain, seek her out! She will agree with every angry point you make and add another twenty reasons why the job sucks! You can count on her to say what everyone is thinking in a staff meeting, and you will be grateful. (NOTE: I think I might be this person.)

Hippie Dippie

This teacher just can't drop that sixties vibe. She wears free-flowing clothes, no bra, dangling jewelry, and has wild hair. She gives spontaneous lectures about the benefits of yoga and suggests that students meditate before and after every class. She speaks very softly, and the peace sign is her go to gesture at all times. She's sweet but annoying and a little stinky.

Repeat Performance

This poor teacher has some kind of speech problem that they are unaware of. They repeat a certain word or noise in between every sentence. The kids actually keep a tally.

Retiring is Not an Option

This teacher should be in a nursing home instead of a school. They have been teaching for 40+ years and can barely even do the job anymore. The kids hate them because they are boring and other teachers hate them because they make three times as much money for doing three times less work. These people usually lecture their classes all day about whatever is on their mind. They are evil geniuses because they make more money than anyone else in the building, and they know they can't be fired, so they don't have to do much more than show up. *Dicks.*

The Thespian

This is usually an English teacher who also runs the theatre department. The theatre is their life. They love to regale anyone who will listen about the various productions they have been in and the D-list actors they have met. They take the school show way too seriously. Directing the middle school performance of "Hello Dolly" is like preparing actors to perform Shakespeare for the Queen of England. Speaking of Shakespeare, no one knows more about him than this person. Just try to stump them! They also attempt to direct a Shakespearean play every now and again, and it is sheer torture for both the students in the play and the adults who have to watch it. Regardless of how ridiculous this person is, you have to appreciate the amount of time they dedicate to the school show- because

I sure as shit ain't staying there til 10 o'clock at night!

OCD

Lord help you if this person is in charge of anything, like a supply closet. They will count everything and hoard supplies. "Do you really need all of those index cards? Here's one pack. Is one pack not enough? How many more do you need? Let's count them out." For fuck's sake lady! They're index cards! This person will also roam around classrooms and offices passing judgment on the poor organizational skills of others. Forget the fact that they totally neglect the actual teaching part of their job because they are too busy organizing the shit out of old folders. If their paperwork is in order, then their life is in order, and everything is going to be okay.

Part-time Teacher, Full-time Douchebag

This person ain't here for the paycheck, and they like to remind everyone of that. They especially like to remind everyone that they are not obligated to attend any meetings or training because they are part-time. Some of them will even brag about how they don't need the money. Well, ain't that fab, you dickbag. If you don't need the money, can I have it?

Too Cool for School

This teacher breaks the cardinal rule of teaching by trying to be everyone's friend. They use the students' slang, and it is downright embarrassing. The students can't get enough of this teacher because instead of doing work they watch SpongeBob videos on YouTube and play on their phones and yet, they still get an A. This person became a teacher because they wanted to stay in high school forever and that is just gross.

Just Here to Coach

This teacher really only cares about coaching their sport but needs to pay the bills. They have zero interest in the subject they teach and don't put in much effort. But put them on the field/court/arena/pit, and the passion and dedication is astounding!

Tacky as F

This lady is truly a marvel. She dresses in clashing neon colors and almost always has sequins somewhere on her body. The version at my school actually takes pieces of hair and gels them down on her cheeks in various patterns. It's wondrous. She almost always wears a rainbow sequin baseball cap with matching rainbow sequin ball earrings and rainbow sequin Keds[i]. She basically doesn't give a fuck what you think. She wears what makes her heart sing, and if you don't like it, you can suck on her sequins.

The DO YOU KNOW WHAT COLLEGE I WENT TO Teacher

This teacher used to be in his high school's magnet program, got a scholarship to a top 10 university for math or science, and is so much smarter than the other teachers that he can't even bear to be in the same room as them. He went to Harvard/Dartmouth/MIT or wherever! He is only here to teach the future brilliant mathematicians of the world and the rest of us peasants should avoid speaking to him unless absolutely necessary.

Cat Lady

Well, this is pretty much as you would imagine: A spinster or widow who owns way too many cats. She is usually wearing cat paraphernalia, and her hair is fluffy and wild like a cat's tail. She smells like cat litter and, god forbid you're around when one of her cats die. You will be forced to mourn for it.

3

EDUSHIT

The principal sent the following email to the staff after spring break:

"How can we expect our students to love school when teachers are already counting how many days until summer? Change your mindset. Start counting how many days you have left to make a difference."

My Response?

"Today, when a student told me that I'm just in a bad mood because I don't get enough dick, I thought, 'Oh no. I only have 96 more days to make a difference in this student's life!'"

"Edushit" is my term for the buzzwords that come and go in the educational world. They are basically complicated ways of describing relatively simple concepts. The only reason you would need to know these terms is if you are preparing for a teaching interview. If you don't throw in at least 5 of these puppies, they will surely think you will be a terrible teacher. (Prior experience? Ideas? Educational philosophy? Discipline practices? Nope! No one gives a shit. But you mention **differentiation** and **scaffolding,** and you are surely the most effective and skilled teacher in the universe!)

Allow me to translate some of the most popular edushit terms:

Common core: The work of state academic leaders who set out to design a benchmark that all states can adopt and follow in their schools.

Translation: Total horseshit (read my 1st book)! There were almost NO teachers on the huge team of "leaders" who created this.

Cohort: A group of people banded together or treated as a group in a program or course of study.

Translation: A super fancy way to say group. The word means group.

Cooperative learning: Placing students into small groups and having them work together toward a common goal.

Translation: The kids are working in groups but realistically 1-2 kids are doing the work while the other 2-3 are drawing dicks on the desktops and watching YouTube.

Critical thinking: The ability to analyze information.

Translation: Something that students used to be able to do before Google was invented.

Differentiation: An instructional technique that is used to reach students with different learning styles. Each student learns best in his own way, and differentiated instruction means that the teacher observes all students to see how he/she can plan instruction that will suit each individual student.

Translation: The snowflakes need more choices to choose from instead of them all doing the same assignment. This is important because in their adult life, they will probably be given just as many choices in the workplace, right?

Extrinsic motivation: When a student is motivated by outside factors or other people.

Translation: The kid is either scared of his parents, or they bribe the shit out of him.

Individual learning styles: The way each individual student learns best. For example, some students are more visual learners, while others are kinesthetic. Teachers can use this theory to figure out how each student learns best, then present their lessons in a way that will suit all learning styles.

Translation: The teacher has to spend a lot more time planning shit.

Interpersonal intelligence: The ability to work effectively with other people.

Translation: The kid is not a dick.

Manipulatives: Handheld objects that help to boost a student's focus in the classroom.

Translation: Toys.

Objective: A statement that describes what students will be able to do upon completion of an instructional experience.

Translation: The thing I have to write on the board that no one ever reads which includes fancy words like "synthesize" and "engage."

Professional development: Specialized training, formal education, or advanced professional learning intended to help administrators, teachers, and other educators improve their professional knowledge, competence, skills, and effectiveness.

Translation: The meetings they force us to go to that can last anywhere from an hour to weeks at a time and are almost always useless and torturous.

Professional learning communities (PLCs): A group of educators that meet regularly, share expertise and work collaboratively to improve teaching skills and the academic performance of students.

Translation: The group they force you to meet with during the precious little planning time you have. The time is mostly spent complaining.

Restorative practices/restorative justice: As opposed to punishing a student for undesirable behavior, restorative practices help build a particular sense of community in which the student feels they are seen, heard, and respected. Usually consists of open dialogue between teacher and students.

Translation: Student tells me to go F myself, but instead of being punished we have to "talk it out" so the student feels heard. Also known as BULLSHIT.

Rigor: Teacher has high expectations and holds all students to the same challenging academic standards and expectations.

Translation: Your class is hard.

Scaffolding: The support that is given to students when a new concept is introduced. In order to best facilitate learning, teachers introduce motivational techniques to pique student interest.

Translation: Fancy schmancy word for steps. Break things up into smaller steps.

Student Progress Monitoring: The teacher sets goals and begins instruction, then he or she measures the student's progress toward meeting those goals each week. With each test, the teacher compares how much the student is expected to have learned to the student's actual rate of learning. The teacher notes the student's performance level and compares it to previous measurements and to expected rates of learning. The teacher tracks the measurements on a graph as a way of showing the success of both the teacher and the student.

Translation: The teacher doesn't ever stop to eat, sleep or even pee because they need every moment to complete this task for 150 students.

Text Complexity: Text complexity refers to how challenging the material is for a student at their specific grade level.

Translation: Is the book hard?

4

TEACHING THE SNAPCHAT GENERATION

"We are wasting our youth

holding cold devices

while we should be holding

one another's warm hands."

-Mohamed Ghazi

When I first started teaching in 2007, most kids did not have a smartphone. We also did not have Smartboards in any of the classrooms. It wasn't hard to hold their attention. A piece of clip art on the overhead projector or a discussion about the pressures of the college application process was enough to keep most of them engaged. Ten years later, the lengths teachers have to go to in order to hold a student's attention are almost comical. Sometimes I feel like a circus monkey, juggling flashy GIFs and funny memes before their eyes, hoping they forget about their phone for two minutes—to little success. More and more, teachers have to personally relate everything to students and make it "hip" in order for kids to care at all. Trying to make Shakespeare cool? Don't even bother with that hip-hop artist who uses Shakespeare as lyrics. They've seen it before, and they're not impressed. Perhaps try pointing out that in Hamlet, when the main character asks to put his head in his girlfriend's lap, he calls it "country matters" which many experts believe is a form of the word cunt! They just might lift their head up and ask what you just said...for a moment. I once had a student tell me that he will never forget that one detail. That's cool, but did he absorb anything else? Who knows.

I feel the pressure to keep everything I do "cool," and it's hard to keep up. But if I don't, I will lose them completely, like many of my much older colleagues. I don't ever want them to view my class as completely useless, and I fear that is how many of them view school in general. Sometimes, no matter how flashy and edgy my lessons are, it still doesn't hold their attention. It can never be as interesting and relevant as the bullshit their friends are posting on snapchat. "Why don't you just take their phones away?" you ask. I often do, and that is the point at which many of them simply put their heads down and cash out. I once even, in a moment of frustration, shouted at a class that I could be showing porn in class, and they would still be looking down at their phones because they have better porn on their own phones! A few kids laughed, and one or two heads popped up. "Did she just say something about...?" But most kept their heads down.

Sometimes when a kid is on their phone, I will just ask them what they are doing.

"Nothing, sorry."

"No seriously, I want to know what is so engrossing. What exactly are you doing?"

9 times out of 10 they are on snapchat, where they post pictures of what they are doing in real time. But what are they doing? Not much.

One time I gave out donuts for whatever reason and at least five kids snapchatted about it immediately. When I'm about to show a movie, many phones come out to document the excitement of movie time. It's ironic that they don't even plan on actually watching the movie.

One time I wanted to reward a class by letting them choose the movie they would watch. I gave them a vote, and it was very heated. They fought adamantly for the film they thought was the most worth watching. When we finally came to a consensus, and I played the film, about 75% of the class began watching their own selections with headphones. I couldn't believe it.

Do I need to be stricter about the phones? Yes. And I have been. And it only caused me health-destroying aggravation. When the administration doesn't have consequences for anything, how can we enforce any rules? I used to have a hanging chart with pockets for each phone. Students would never voluntarily put their phones in the pocket. I would have to argue with each student, separately, about the phones at the beginning of each class. Some students are so protective of their phones that it mirrors a physical addiction. If you try to take away their drug, they react like a drug addict who can't get their next fix. I couldn't take the frustration anymore.

To be fair, if admin actually tried to discipline kids for the phone situation, there would be long lines of angry students pouring into the office all day long. They don't have the resources to handle that.

The phone addiction is so extreme that it might be one of the main reasons I do not want to teach anymore. Phones and social media have crept their way into every aspect of a teenager's life. Remember when you had to work up the nerve to ask someone out? Now you just "slide into their DMs (direct messages)." Remember when you had to have the balls to call someone's house and ask their mom if they could talk? Now you send a text any time, day or night. Remember that time you talked to your crush for hours on the phone until you finally built up the nerve to talk in person or go on a date? Now you text, send emojis and comment on pics. Sending someone a direct message on social media is actually considered to be pretty ballsy these days. Can you imagine? The way kids interact is completely different than it has ever been, and it will inevitably change our world. It already has.

5

YOUR ASS IS GETTING HUGE AND OTHER THINGS KIDS SAID TO ME WHEN I WAS PREGNANT

"If you're pregnant with a girl baby

and you have sex,

can the baby get pregnant?"

-A question from one of my sophomores

My answer was,

"Yeah, I think so."

I think it is cruel to expect a pregnant woman to work if she doesn't want to. It is a precious and difficult time, both physically and emotionally. It is a lot to ask a gestating woman to handle the various stressful tasks that come with many jobs, but to expect a woman to cope with teaching 100-200 adolescent minds while pregnant? That is just cruel.

Teaching is not the kind of job where you can hide your head in a trashcan behind your desk or run to the bathroom to vomit as needed. You are "on" all day long. And when you're pregnant, your condition becomes the only thing the students can focus on. Every time they look at your belly they remember what act must have taken place to get that baby in there. This inevitably leads to extraordinarily inappropriate questions and comments. Kids seem to lack the mental editing equipment that prevents them from asking their teacher if they still have sex while pregnant (yes, a kid asked me that). They also don't understand why the teacher is so insulted by these queries. They're just curious, Miss!

As if unending nausea and vomiting for three months aren't enough. As if stretch marks and hanging skin flaps aren't enough. As if weight gain, a constant need to urinate, weird cramps, acid reflux, heartburn, skin tags, insomnia and hormonal mood swings aren't enough to deal with… here are 150 fifteen-year-olds to babysit! And oh yeah, teach them Shakespeare and stuff too!

Here are some of the things students have said to me during my two pregnancies:

They love to give you daily updates on your size.

"You're getting bigger."

"It's so big."

"You're not that big."

"Shouldn't it be bigger?"

And yes, one even said to me, "Your ass is getting bigger!"

When I shot her a look, she responded, "What! It's a compliment!"

"Your boobs are getting *huge!*"

"You must be having a girl because when it's a boy, it sticks out like a basketball, but when it's a girl, you just get fat all over."

They love to tell you their plans for procreation.

"I'm not gonna have my baby when I'm old. I'm having my babies when I'm 19!"

"All these old teachers are getting pregnant. I'm having mine young!"

"My boyfriend graduates next year, and we're gonna have a baby!"

They feel the need to tell you their own birth story.

"I was born on a couch! My mom sat down, and my head came out!"

"My mom had to have 17 stitches in her poonanie cuz of me!"

"My mom said poop came out when she was having me!"

"When my mom's water broke my dad slipped in it and hit his head!"

They have great suggestions for names.

After they just began offering them up, unprompted, I asked my students to write down a few suggestions for baby names. Here are my favorites:

Tupac, Sexi, Lil Uzzi, Tequila, Money, Areola, Kween, Lil Teach, Cinderella, Starbuck, Trucker, K8 (Kate), Strawberry, LaQueefa, Saytan, Pepsi, Phelony, Elizabit, Nylon, Daddy, Kurrency, and my personal favorite Fartisha.

They ask insanely stupid and/or improper questions.

"Do people have sex when they're pregnant?"

"Are you afraid to have that baby? It's gonna, like, *destroy* your vag!" *The kid actually raised his hand during a lesson to ask this very necessary question.*

"Does it rip all the way down to your butthole?"

"Can you get it sewn back up, so it's tight again?"

"Can other people drink breast milk, besides the baby?"

"I can tell you what you're having. What position were you in? Were you on top?"

"So the baby eats all the food you eat and drinks everything you drink? It's disgusting."

"Do you get those hanging things in your butt? My mom did."

"Why are you still fat after you have the baby?"

"Can you get pregnant from a hot tub?"

"Are you afraid that you'll sit down to poop and the baby will come out in the toilet?"

"Can you get pregnant from a dog?"

FOR FUCK'S SAKE, HAVEN'T THESE KIDS HEARD OF GOOGLE!?

A student asked me how many months pregnant I was. A few minutes after I told him he stood up and announced, "September! She had sex in September!"

Another strange aspect of being pregnant while teaching is that some of your students might be expecting too! During my first pregnancy, I had two pregnant students and an 11th grader with a 3-year-old son. I would try to connect with them sometimes, but they never really seemed bothered by the pregnancy the way I was.

"Aren't you tired?" I would ask. "Not really," they'd reply.

"Aren't you scared?" I asked. "Not really," they'd answer.

For some reason, this baby stuff was much more troublesome for me!

6

BUTT CHUGGING AND OTHER FUN ACTIVITIES

"Imagine unrolling a condom and
stuffing it up one side of your nose,
then plugging the other nostril and
inhaling until the long piece of latex
slides into your throat.
Then you reach back there
with your fingers and pull it
from your mouth.

Why would someone do that?"

-Washington Post

In my first book I talked about some of the strange and idiotic games that adolescents play, such as Sack Tapping (where students smash each other in the genitals over and over, which has led to testicles needing to be surgically removed) and Rappelling (where students jump off a building and the one with the most severe injury wins). I didn't think the games could get more stupid or dangerous, but then I started noticing the "online challenge" phenomena. These challenges involve doing something remarkably unsafe and filming it for YouTube. Some of these challenges are so alarming that even WebMD has articles warning parents about them. To make sure we are all up to date on these insane games, I have briefly summarized them below:

The Tide Pod Challenge

According to the New York Times, "teens are biting down on brightly colored laundry detergent packets and spitting out or ingesting its contents, an act that poses serious health risks."[ii] What's the point? Filming it for attention on social media of course! Apparently, it has been a long-running joke online that the detergent pods resemble candy and look delicious. I'm sure that is perfectly true for a toddler. But anyone over the age of 5 should know better. In the first two weeks of 2018, poison control centers handled 39 cases in which teenagers were intentionally exposed to the detergent packets.[iii] The chemicals cause severe burns to the mouth, esophagus or respiratory tract, and some people have even died as a result of eating the packets. But it's all about the number of likes. *Give yourself chemical burns to your esophagus for the likes.*

The Choking Game

I thought this was an urban myth, but apparently, this is a real thing. Kids choke each other until they experience a brief "high" and pass out. The problem is, when you choke someone, they often die. A fascinating, but in no way surprising, part of this story is that 87% of those who have died from this game are boys. (I'm pretty sure most of the kids engaging in most of the games I describe are boys as well. I'm not trying to be sexist. Facts are facts and teenaged males have brain damage.)

The Cinnamon Challenge

Look up "cinnamon challenge" on YouTube, and you will get 1.6 million videos of kids swallowing a spoonful of cinnamon. What makes it so difficult, and dangerous, is that it immediately dries out your throat, causing extreme coughing fits. Some kids have been hospitalized and placed on ventilators from cinnamon getting into their lungs. *Cool!*

Butt-chugging

This is not as disgusting as it sounds, but it is definitely stupid. Basically, kids pour alcohol into each other's buttholes because apparently, you get drunk quicker that way. Just picture kids stealing your vodka bottle and sticking them in each other's B-holes. Yeah, I take back what I originally said. This *is* as disgusting as it sounds.

Condom snorting

This bullshit is exactly what it sounds like. You snort a condom up one nostril and pray to god that it comes out of the other one. If it doesn't, it's probably stuck in your face somewhere, or about to choke you to death.

The Fire Challenge

Just when you think these games couldn't get any dumber, you read that kids are actually setting themselves on fire. And you shed a tear for humanity. What's the point of this challenge? Well, after you pour flammable liquids on yourself and set yourself on fire, your friends upload a video of the whole thing to social media while you suffer second or third-degree burns and sometimes lung damage. *But it's worth it if you get a few likes, ain't it bruh?*

The Duct Tape Challenge

For this bit of after school amusement, one must bind his friend with duct tape, either to himself or to a stationary object, like a pole. Then the friend must struggle to break free. If it sounds relatively harmless, consider the fact that many kids use electric tape and wind up ripping off layers of skin. There was one young man who fell and split his head open while trying to break free. He came very close to having permanent brain damage. *Lit.*

Human Piñata

It's a pretty simple game, but not for the faint of heart. This is where you punch and/or kick another person until one of the following comes out of them: tears, snot, vomit, or blood.

Bottle Flipping Challenge

Seemingly harmless, in 2016, the compulsion promoted through online videos to toss a partly filled plastic bottle and try to get it to land upright captivated children across the country. The craze started with a YouTube video of a school talent show. A contestant flipped a water bottle, which landed upright on the table. The crowd went nuts. That clip has been viewed *more than six million times*, and millions of kids sought to recreate the same video clip. While this activity might seem fairly safe, the danger lies in a nearby adult strangling a kid who has flipped a bottle one too many times.

The Panty Challenge

While not likely to cause injury, this challenge is Dumb with a capital D. Essentially a female pulls down her undies and snaps a shot of the crotch area to prove that there is no discharge present. Make sure to post the photo to social media! Just having to think about and type the word "discharge" is unnerving. What is the point of this? Vagina shaming! A little sludge in the panties is a perfectly natural occurrence, and this "challenge" is merely perpetuating the idea that things that happen naturally are gross. And sometimes they are, but gross stuff is part of life! How do you think you were conceived and brought forth into the world, kids? I can assure you that it was gross!

The "In My Feelings"/Kiki Challenge

On June 29, 2018, a comedian named Shiggy shared a video of himself dancing (or "doing the shiggy") in the street to Drake's lyrics. For some unknown reason, the video went viral, and hundreds of thousands of videos popped up of people recreating the same dance moves in various settings. Celebrities participated too. It was all quite harmless until the teenaged brain got involved. People started jumping into traffic to do the dance. "One teen fractured her skull after attempting the challenge at a roundabout. One woman was robbed as she concentrated on her moves, while other oblivious dancers have tripped over potholes." [iv] One person danced directly into a lamppost. The challenge became so dangerous that Turkey started giving out fines, and in Egypt, you can be jailed for up to a year.

Safer Alternatives:

The Don't Touch Each Other Challenge

This is a very difficult game. It involves kids going the entire day without touching each other. I bet most can't make it past 10 minutes.

The Complaining Challenge

The rules of this game are simple but very difficult to master. You must go an entire school day without complaining, not even once. I've tried it a few times, but I've never won.

The Sit-Down and Shut the Fuck Up Challenge

None of my students have won the challenge yet.

7

WORSE THAN WORKING WITH RABID RACCOONS

"I was a military artillery observer
(responsible for directing artillery
and mortar fire onto a target.)
I student taught for 2 semesters,
then switched majors.
I don't know how anyone does that job."
-former student teacher

I'm sure by now you have gathered that teaching is extremely stressful. But do you really understand just *how* stressful it is? I scoured the internet for research on teachers and stress, and I did not find much. But what I did find was even worse than I had imagined.

According to a survey conducted by the American Federation of Teachers in 2017, 58% of their respondents said their mental health was "not good" for seven or more of the previous 30 days. That is a 24% increase from two years earlier. They also don't appear to get much sleep: only 1 in 5 get 8 or more hours of sleep per night.

In a 2015 survey, 30,000 educators reported often feeling emotionally and physically exhausted at the end of the day. Nearly two-thirds, or 61 percent, of educators, find work "always" or "often" stressful, twice the rate of workers of other professions. 27% of educators said they have been threatened, bullied or harassed, versus 7% of employed adults in the general population. When asked who the bully was, 35% identified a principal, administrator or supervisor, and 50% said it was a student.

100% of the 30,000 teachers surveyed by the American Federation of Teachers "agreed" or "strongly agreed" that they were enthusiastic about the profession when they began their careers, yet only 53% still felt enthusiastic at the point in their careers when they took the survey. Those who "strongly agreed" dropped from 89% to just 15%.

A recent survey by TES, one of the biggest online teaching communities in the world, showed that teachers work more unpaid overtime than any other profession, with 61% of teachers working as many as 13 extra hours every week.

Attrition is high, and enrollment in teacher preparation programs has fallen some 35% over the past five years — a decrease of nearly 240,000 teachers in all.

I decided to conduct my own research online and had over 10,000 responses from teachers around the world. 92% agreed that teaching negatively affects their sleeping habits, with 31% saying they have trouble sleeping most school nights. 78% said that teaching negatively affects their health. 74% worry about their personal safety at school. 93% said that teaching is the most stressful job they have ever had (these responders included teachers who have been EMTs, lawyers, and various other stressful jobs). 70% agreed that teaching gets harder every year. Only 13% feel they can live comfortably on their salary. 26% constantly worry about supporting themselves and 1% actually qualify for welfare.

Only 4% feel they can comfortably support their family with their teaching salary, 50% of responders with a family to support constantly worry about money and 2.5% of their families qualify for welfare.

Only 25% feel a general sense of respect from students, only 19% from parents and only 29% from administrators.

Only 19% of the 10,000 teachers surveyed say they have *never* regretted becoming a teacher.

So what do they do to cope?

41% responded that they took sleeping pills because of their teaching job.

68% admitted to caffeine addiction due to teaching, while only 10% said they did not need it.

23% have taken antidepressants specifically because of teaching, while 16% are considering it.

29% have had to go an anti-anxiety medication because of teaching, and 26% are considering it.

73% drink alcohol to cope with the stress of teaching, 9% drink on most school nights.

18% smoke marijuana to cope with the stress (I suspect that more teachers would if they could afford it or if it was legal).

Some people would argue that teachers start teaching young, and haven't had the chance to work other stressful jobs. So I asked my social media followers to describe other stressful jobs and situations they have worked that still don't compare to the stress of teaching.

I worked at a crisis center where people in crisis would call or come by. They were often suicidal. It was very difficult, but not as stressful as teaching! At least at the crisis center, I was only handling one person at a time. As a teacher, I take care of 150+ students a day, and many are in crisis.

Here are other's responses:

"Teaching is more stressful than working at a wildlife rehab where I regularly handled, fed and cleaned lizards, snakes, raccoons, owls, hawks, and bobcats. Some were rabid."

"Teaching is more stressful than being the only cook in a kitchen making breakfast for 150 customers."

"Teaching is more stressful than working in the medical field for 18 years and touching things that would blow people's minds. I was a teacher for one year, and it was heinous. It was too stressful to relay information and keep people engaged. I would never try it again."

"Teaching is more stressful than cleaning up a construction site for 13 hours a day 6 days a week. I was physically exhausted, but not mentally and emotionally. Plus, I didn't think about work when I went home."

"Teaching is more stressful than my first bowel movement after giving birth."

"Teaching is more stressful than working for Child Protective Services. At least they provided whatever supplies I needed."

"Teaching is more stressful than being a guard in a jail."

"Teaching is more stressful than being a park ranger at a National Park. I was bluff charged by a bear. Still not as stressful as teaching."

"Teaching is more stressful than undergoing spinal surgery that could have paralyzed me."

"When I brought home my first baby, and my milk never came in, she caught respirator virus and lost 2 pounds, then was allergic to all formula and she was colic and didn't sleep over an hour at a time for 2 months! My last 5 years of teaching? Still harder!"

"Teaching is more stressful than accounting multi-million dollar accounts."

"Teaching is more stressful than carrying troughs of brick mortar in the hot sun for 8 hours a day. I was so tired when I got home that I had to nap, so I had the energy just to shower! However, I didn't have to worry about those bricks once I left work."

"Teaching is more stressful than being a line cook where sometimes the chef would throw pans, and I cut my fingertip off."

"Teaching is more stressful than working as Chuck E. Cheese and getting groped by creepy adults. It doesn't pay much more either."

"Teaching is more stressful than working at a supermarket and getting robbed at gunpoint twice."

"Teaching is more stressful than giving birth to an 11-pound baby with no meds!"

"I'm an ER Nurse, and I bow humbly before every teacher."

"I danced in the Disneyland Parade as Mickey in 100-degree heat, and I wasn't allowed to take the head off even when I vomited from heat exhaustion. Teaching is worse."

"Teaching is more stressful than scaffolding 800ft in the air while people are walking below you."

"Teaching is more stressful than flying a low-level helicopter route through mountains with the newest kid in the squadron and making sure we don't die."

"I am a firefighter. I taught once a week for a year at a high school and teaching is definitely more stressful than being a firefighter."

"I left teaching to become a doctor, and I can honestly tell you that teaching is harder than med school."

"Teaching is more stressful than working clean up after Hurricane

Katrina."

"Teaching is more stressful than working as a customer service agent in baggage claim for United Airlines. Anytime someone's luggage went missing; I would have to try to locate it. One time a dog escaped from the pit of an airplane and was hit by a 767 on the runway, and I had to deliver the news to the owners. Teaching is worse."

"Teaching is more stressful than being a naturalist educator which included cleaning hawk shit and regurgitation off the walls and having them fly at your face when you bring them dead mice."

Other respondents cited the following jobs as less stressful than teaching: oncology nurse, debt collector, probation officer, police officer, 911 dispatcher, lifeguard, bounty hunter, bartender on New Year's Eve, lawyer, and working on Black Friday at Target, Best Buy, Kmart and Toys "R" Us.

Don't believe it? You must not be a teacher.

8

ATTACK OF THE UNFIREABLE BATSHIT CRAZY TEACHERS

"It's beautiful thing to see person smiling,

but beautiful to see educate."

From *Courageous & Freedom:*

My Journeying to Greatness

(Written by Sir Harry Baals,

the substitute teacher who always

fills in for me)

Let me make this very clear right away: I am absolutely FOR teachers' unions. However, there is one glaring issue with them, and that is what I will be focusing on. But I am so afraid that people will take my criticism of unions as fuel to fight against them, that I am first going to explain *why we need them.*

When we talk about reforming schools, the first thing that always comes up is how we can hold on to the good teachers and get rid of the bad ones. Unions dictate how you can (or, more often, cannot) get rid of shitty teachers, so people immediately take issue with them. But we can't just get rid of unions altogether. Here's why:

The National Education Association (NEA) was created in 1857 for the main purpose of increasing teachers' salaries across the nation. Teachers' pay was extraordinarily low (like way lower than it is today if you can effin believe that) despite the increasing workload and demands. Teachers were leaving in droves (sound familiar?) mostly for this reason, and the NEA sought to fix this problem. The NEA also did other important things like advocate for integrated classrooms and fight against child labor.

Currently, teachers' unions protect basic fundamental rights for both teachers and students. They defend their first amendment rights. They ensure equal pay and fair working conditions (because believe me, if school districts could pile on 50 more job responsibilities for no extra pay, THEY WOULD), and they even fight for safe and healthy working conditions (like clean air and asbestos-free buildings). Unions also fight for smaller class sizes and adequate funding. Districts in the U.S. without unions have even more overcrowded classes and starting salaries as low as $26,000. It is hard for them to find college graduates who are willing to teach on a cashier's salary. If over 50% of teachers quit in their first 5 years despite the presence of unions, imagine how many would leave if unions were destroyed? It is also interesting to note that the five states where teachers' unions are illegal also have the lowest student test scores.

There are many more reasons why unions are essential in education, but I'll let you research that on your own. Now on to the misery. I am going to focus on the one infuriating aspect of teachers' unions: how impossible they make it to get rid of batshit crazy teachers.

I have worked with hundreds of teachers, and the great majority of them are unbelievably dedicated, hardworking, and effective. But every school has two or three insane and/or completely useless teachers that they just can't seem to get rid of. And it is important for you to know that every other staff member in the building hates their guts. We despise these people because they make our whole profession look bad. They make the same amount of money as us (or in some cases much, much more because they are really old and won't retire) and yet they do nothing besides show up. Let me revise that. Some don't even bother to show up but are masters at producing doctor's notes and other various excuses.

Why is it so hard to get rid of these nutjobs, you ask? Let me briefly explain. These cases often end up having to be fought over in court, and that can be very costly as well as time-consuming. But the main thing that makes it so difficult to complete the process of getting a teacher fired is that it requires so much work by administration that it basically becomes their full-time job. Let's say a teacher named Billy Bob has been coming in late, leaving early, and does nothing but show Disney movies in class. He must be observed between six and ten times in a very specific time period and receive poor evaluations on all of them. The problem with this is that Billy Bob knows how to play this little game and he teaches an actual lesson when he is being observed. But let's just say that Billy Bob bombs all of his observations. Next, an impartial observer must come in to observe him. If they don't see a problem with Billy Bob, then the case is dismissed, and the process must start all over again. If the observer does find Billy Bob problematic, then a "consulting teacher" is brought in to coach Billy Bob into being a better teacher. Next, a "remediation plan" is written for the following year and Billy Bob must be evaluated on three more occasions to determine if the plan worked. If the principal determines that the plan did not work the process enters a "pre-hearing." A few months later, hearing officers must be chosen but can then be rejected by either side, and new ones must be selected. A few months after that comes the hearing which requires transcripts, post-hearing briefs, and recommendations. Then the Board of Education decides whether or not to fire Billy Bob. If they decide to fire him, the teacher can then appeal the decision. *(Are you still reading this?)* Over the next year, a court reviews the Board's decision. If the court upholds the decision to fire him Billy Bob can appeal to the state's Supreme Court next. It could take another year for the Supreme Court to make a ruling.

SOOOOOO... considering how ridiculous a process it is to get rid of a teacher, most administrators take a short-term approach and transfer the teacher to another school. At least they don't have to deal with their crazy ass anymore. And that is how shitty teachers get passed around like a game of hot potato.

My whole point in bringing this up (I'm getting to the funny part, I swear) is to highlight how miserable it is for all of the amazing, hardworking teachers to have to tolerate these crazy a-holes. Here are a few examples of the nutjobs I have had to work with:

The Crazy Bunny Lady

This woman was actually arrested for animal cruelty for keeping dozens of rabbits in her backyard during the winter. They all froze/starved to death, and there were a few they found in her home that were beaten to death. This made me want to smash her face in because I love and value animals as much as people. (My dogs share my pillow at night, and we spoon.) You might think that a person who was convicted of animal cruelty would be deemed incapable of teaching children, but you would be wrong. She continued "teaching" for many years, despite the students who threw mini carrots at her and yelled, "Bunny killer!" in the hallways. It wasn't just her cruel treatment of animals that made her unfit; she also had genuine mental issues. She would get in heated arguments with herself and yell at people who were not actually there. For years the administration tried to get rid of her unsuccessfully until one day she told a quiet class to go eff themselves and walked out the front door of the school never to return. Sometimes these things just work themselves out.

Mr. Norman Bates

I wish I could tell you the real name of this man because it is the exact name of a fictional serial killer. To achieve the same effect, I'll call him Norman Bates.

Norman had a thick, mysterious accent. It was like a mix of French, German, Jamaican and a bit drunk. Seriously, no one knew where the eff this guy was from, and every time you asked him he would flash you a look of shock and yell, "I am America of course!"

He was entertaining to be around if you didn't have to work with him. He was extremely loud and dramatic about *everything*. He was assigned to work with another teacher in my department who I'll call Shirley, the poor thing. Several times a day he would bust the door open and stalk around the staff lounge screaming, "Shirley! Where is Shirley! I *need* to have Shirley! Shirley!" If Shirley was present she would slowly sink down in her seat until he noticed her and then he would stand over her and scream a long rant about various things he was upset about such as the quality of the soap in the men's bathroom. If Shirley was not present, he would demand to know her whereabouts. While I thought the whole thing was hilarious, most people wanted to murder him. Besides being loud and a bit nutty, Norman rarely came to class. He would often just skip school altogether. However, any time the administration called him in for questioning about this, he would somehow produce a doctor's note with a brand new illness. After a few years, Norman had suffered from irritable bowel syndrome, anxiety, rheumatoid arthritis, high blood pressure, gout, Lyme disease, migraines, heart failure (yes, heart failure), carpal tunnel syndrome, asthma, seizures and he had been hit by a car four times. Every time they asked him to recount the details of the same car accident, the details would change and get more and more hilarious. As amusing as he was, Norman was eventually transferred to another school, and then another. He's probably coming to your school next. Enjoy!

B.C. Teacher

How effin old *is* this guy anyway? I am in no way trying to commit age discrimination. Some older teachers have been doing this shit forever (but why though!?) and continue to be amazing at it! But other old ass teachers have been teaching since Moses was in Egypt Land and they need to do everyone a favor and ride that sweet retirement package into a lovely Floridian sunset.

My school has one man in particular who has been teaching at the same school for 55 years. This guy doesn't even teach. He hands out the same worksheets that he typed on a typewriter half a century ago and then lectures while the students take a little snooze. He is part of a salary program that was drastically cut five different times throughout his career, but he still gets this insane amount of money because he got in during a time when there was almost no cap on salaries. He once printed out a pay stub and left it on the printer, and it almost incited a riot. This dude is a *baller*. Another important aspect of his story is that his contract is from a time when a teacher would retire and continue to make almost the same salary. *Do you understand what I'm telling you?* He could make pretty much the same amount of money and not have to come to work ever again! Most teachers today have to work until they physically can't anymore because they will only receive a fraction of their monthly salary. So what the eff is wrong with this person? It has been speculated that he is a childless widower and would be lonely and bored. I can understand that, but be reasonable! Take that money and go travel the world! Rescue 50 dogs! Go shopping! Take some classes! *Have some sense!* Someone once asked him if he would ever retire and he said, "I will die here." One time he fell asleep at his desk, and I thought, "He called it!"

Bumps on a Log

Every school has a handful of bumps on a log. These are teachers or paraeducators who show up on time and stay the whole day, but that's the extent of what they do. They are fairly harmless, but they also *do nothing*. A lot of the time the person is extremely old but just isn't ready to give up their full paycheck. (Plus, if they've been in the system long enough they are making some pretty sweet cash for doing diddly squat.) In my experience, the bumps on a log have mostly been Special Education teachers, who were trained long before inclusion classes were created. (Special Ed. teachers- just stop right there! I am IN NO WAY trying to say that these people are representative of you in general! Most of you are very hardworking, dedicated and necessary teachers. But you know as well as I do, that a few of your colleagues don't do shit but make you all look bad, just like the shitty mainstream teachers. *So calm down, okay?*)

The reason it is easier for a Special Ed. teacher to get away with their blob-like behavior is because they do not have to run the class directly. It is called a "co-teaching" situation, and they are there to help the Special Ed. kids. So if they don't show up on time or do jack shit in class, it isn't particularly noticeable because the subject teacher still runs the class.

Substitute Creatures

I can't believe how many disclaimers I have to write in this chapter! Here we go again: Not all substitute teachers are useless, irresponsible or crazy. Some are _____, _____ and even _____ (fill in appropriate positive adjectives.) But many are indeed useless, irresponsible and/or crazy.

Being a substitute teacher can be a very easy job if you get a good group of students who are willing to listen. It can also be a total nightmare if they view you as having no authority. I have been a daily sub and a long-term sub, so I have experienced it all. However, despite the circumstances, I still dressed properly, showed up on time, kept my shoes and socks on, stayed awake, spoke appropriately to the students, and tried to implement the lesson the teacher left. You know, the bare minimum of professionalism. (Okay one time the VHS— *remember those?*--tape the teacher left was jumping a lot, so I shut it off, and we told ghost stories in the dark. The teacher was not happy. Sorry, not sorry.)

The subs I've had have often turned the class into their own personal soapbox where they lecture the class on whatever is important to them. Sometimes these are useful lectures, like the one Mr. Harry Baals gives each and every time he is called upon to sub. The gist of Mr. Baals' lecture is the importance of education. He takes up the entire class period talking about how important it is to get your schoolwork done *while impeding students from doing that very thing*. Next, he passes around his self-published memoir called *Courageous & Freedom: My Journeying to Greatness,* and shows them where they can buy their own copy online. The last few minutes of class are spent watching videos of him driving his cab on YouTube (I don't know why). When teachers complain that this sub *never* does the lesson plan they've left, they are told that he is one of the best subs we have. He has no criminal background, shows up on time, and is always available last minute. They are right. This is one of the best. Others come late, leave early, don't show up, don't speak *a word* of English, get in loud fights in foreign languages on their phones, eat smelly meals during class, take their shoes and socks off and/or sleep in class. A subbing job isn't the most lucrative gig in the world, but the pay and conditions ain't half bad. *So why can't they find any normal people to do it?*

Other Nutjobs

I once again turned to my teacher followers to describe the nutjobs they've had to work with who just couldn't be fired. Here are my favorites:

"Sub used to get so mad at students that he threw desks and chairs at them. The principal said it was okay because the kids needed to learn a lesson, even if it meant avoiding flying objects."

"An older male teacher told me he liked when I wore sandals because he could see more of my feet and he was into that."

"A teacher used to speak in tongues when the students misbehaved. She would scream, 'Oh Lord Jay-sus!' and start babbling indecipherably. You could hear her down the hallway."

"We had an openly racist, homophobic teacher. The school tried to get rid of him, but parents voted to reinstate him because he gave every student an A!"

"My co-teacher pushed me off a chair because I didn't pick her to help chaperone a field trip to a circus. During a fire drill, she pushed a kid in a wheelchair outside and then left him there. It took hours to locate him."

"I worked with a kindergarten teacher who would turn off the lights, pack up her stuff, and sit at a table with her bag and purse in her lap, meditating with her eyes closed for the last hour of class time. The kids would go crazy hiding in closets, crawling over desks, running around screaming and she completely ignored them."

"We have a crazy art teacher who brings in insane things for the kids to draw. She went to a farm and rented a goat for them to draw, and it shit all over the hallways."

"What about the teacher who shot YouTube videos in class about being a 29-year-old virgin?"

"A teacher drove her truck onto the lawn in front of her classroom and had the students wash it. She helped too, in her bikini top and shorts."

"A teacher used to look under the boys' desks to check for boners."

"One teacher took the whole week of Thanksgiving off. The following week she announced that she had taken the days off to cook for us, and she filled the staff fridge with Thanksgiving food. She brought the receipts to the principal for reimbursement."

"During a staff meeting, a teacher announced that she had been diagnosed with a new ailment (she had many). This one was a 'petrified vagina.' "

"A teacher I used to work with told the boys that erections were works of the devil and if a boy ever got one he should tell it that it is an instrument of evil and that it is not welcome. She also splashed holy water on students and handed out prayer cards. Certain students were told to pray to 'ungayify' themselves. Yet she has tenure, and I don't."

"A teacher was arrested for drunk driving his four-wheeler and pulling a gun on a car full of kids. He told the cops to hurry up because he is a science teacher and he had to be at school in the morning. He was gone for the rest of the year, but he's back this year!"

"I was told that because I was a new teacher, I had to work with an assistant who was experienced in behavior management. She would get into screaming matches with the kids, and I started to realize they put her in my class because no one else would work with her. During class, she would often hide in the storage cupboard, and when I peeked in, she was eating a whole raw onion and a full chili pepper. It came out that her water bottle was full of vodka, but she still wasn't fired."

"Once on a field trip, a crazy kindergarten teacher asked me how many kids she is supposed to have. I told her that I only knew how many were in my own class. She shrugged as we got onto the bus to go home. 15 minutes later we got a call that two students were left behind. The woman went nuts yelling at me that it was my fault. We had to stop traffic to turn around on the highway."

Nutjob Teachers in the News

The following are real news headlines:

Drunk Teacher Urinated on Himself in Front of Students

Teacher Deflates Student's Tires after Finding Car in Spot

SC Middle School Teacher Accused of Slapping Student

Teacher Orders Student to Unclog Toilet with Bare Hands

Teacher Stuffs 11 Kids in Car, 2 in the Trunk, and Takes them to Walmart for Snacks

Police: Teacher Showed up to Work Plastered and Pantless

Teacher Accused of Fighting Teen

Cops: Teacher Arrested After Cartwheel with No Panties

Canadian Teacher Accused of Telling Students Inappropriate Things, Including "grow some balls" and "lick me where I fart"

Elementary School Teachers Accused Of Forcing Students to Fight

Florida PE Teacher Suspended After Allegedly Giving Students Twerking Lessons

Teacher Shaves Student's Armpit in Class

Teacher Says 'Higher Power' Told Him to Attack Kid on Skateboard

Houston Teacher Caught with 53 Pounds of Marijuana in Car

Teacher was Arrested for Drunkenly Letting a 14-year-old boy Drive Her to Waffle House

The Pooperintendent: Someone Was repeatedly defecating on a New Jersey High School's Sports Field. It Was the Superintendent

Before you judge the preceding teachers consider the following real headlines:

Student Charged After Teacher Eats Pot Brownie

4th Graders Plotted to Kill Teacher with Hand Sanitizer, Cops Say

12-Year-Old Girl Accused of Trying to Kill Mother: Teen Upset Mother Took Away Her iPhone

Teen Sentenced for Vomiting on Teacher

Teacher's Aide Suspended for Yawning Near School Principal

High School Boys Trick Female Economics Teacher into Eating Semen

Poet: I Can't Answer Questions on Standardized Tests about My Own Poems

Disrespect Caught on Tape: Student Blows Cigar Smoke in Teacher's Face

Two 10-Year-Old Pupils Tried to Poison Their Teacher by Spiking Her Coffee with Toxic Fluid

Republican Lawmaker to Teachers: If You Want a Better Life, Get a Second Job

Teacher Left Unconscious after Vicious Assault by Student's Mom

A Primary School closed its Doors Indefinitely after an Elderly Teacher was Brutally Assaulted

Teen Arrested After Trying to Hire a Clown to Kill Her Teacher

Woman Charged with Throwing Lighter Fluid on Son's Teacher, Threatening to Burn Down School

Student Douses Self with Gasoline

Teen Myths: Mountain Dew & Marijuana as Pregnancy Prevention

Student Arrested in February for Threatening to Blow up School- Maintains it was a Fart Joke

U.S. Student who Electrocuted his Nipples Sues Teacher for Not Warning Him it was Dangerous

After reading those headlines, arriving drunk and pantless to work doesn't seem that farfetched, does it?

9

WHY I CAN'T TEACH LITTLE KIDS

"I'll die if you touch me."
-Vladimir Nabokov

You know that one kid who is always in desperate need of an antibiotic? Let me tell you a little story. A while ago I taught drama at a day camp. (It wasn't real drama, because the kids were ages 2-10. It was more of a dramatic game of pass the bean bag.) So, one of the little ones had that yellow-green snot situation all the time. One day she decided to go around hugging everyone. She took a running start towards me, and my instinct was to move out of the way. She ran headfirst into a tree. She started screaming and had a huge dent on her forehead but, thankfully, no one saw what had happened. I said, "She just ran headfirst into a tree! I don't know why!" Afterward, another counselor came up to me and said, "I saw what happened and I would have done the same thing."

Bottom line: If you're not my kid, I don't want you to touch me. I care about you, but I don't love you. Not enough to get your boogers on me. And that is why I don't teach little kids.

10

NEVER ENDING SHIT PARADES

(Parent Teacher Conferences)

"Great teachers will never be able

to make up for bad parents,

nor should they be expected to."

-Taylor Mali

When a parent conference is called for a high schooler, it is usually not for a good reason. The kid is failing multiple classes, not coming to class and/or being a giant pain in the ass. Anyone from any walk of life can procreate, so as the teacher, you really don't know what type of situation you are about to be a part of. Will the parent try to defend their kid's shitty behavior? Will they call the teacher a liar? Will they regale the group with weird sex stories? Anything is possible. The parent can pretty much say whatever they feel in the moment (like their kid) while the teacher is expected to maintain a completely professional demeanor. It is one of the most challenging parts of the job, especially when confronted with the following true life situations:

Teacher: "Thank you for coming today Mrs. Cobbledick. As you know-"

Mom: "Is that your wedding picture? You know I got a personal trainer before *my* wedding."

Teacher: "Your son has only come to class twice this entire semester. I don't see why I should provide all of that makeup work."

Mom: "You've really been a bitch since you got married, so maybe it isn't working out. But you can't take it out on the students."

Dad: *"You're Ms. Morris?* But my son said you were good looking!"

Counselor: "We called this meeting because your daughter is failing all of her classes."

Mom *(as three-year-old lifts up her shirt and starts sucking on her braless breast):* "Not now Chip! Mommy is talking!"

Chip (fighting with mom for boob): "But I want it! I want! I want!"

Mom: "Fine. Make it quick!"

(The following year the same mom changed her kid's shitty diaper on the conference table.)

Mom & Dad: *(stinking of alcohol and carrying coke bottles full of whiskey):* "Now what is this about!"

Teacher: "Your son skips class half of the time and, when he *does* show up, he does not do any work and is extremely disruptive."

Dad *(as Mom conspicuously rubs his crotch under the table):* "So?"

Teacher: "So it makes it difficult for me to teach the other students."

Mom *(laughing):* "Ain't that like *your job?*"

Teacher: "Yes, teaching is my job. But your son makes it impossible."

Dad *(also having a great time):* "Well this sounds to me like it's *your* problem and not *mine!*"

Creepy Dad *(looking the teacher up and down inappropriately):* "Happy belated Valentine's day! I see why my son behaves in your class!"

Teacher: "We are having a lot of trouble with your son using inappropriate language at school."

Parent: "Well I don't know where the fuck he hears language like that."

Teacher: "I am very concerned about your granddaughter. She currently has a 9% in my class. Despite her being 17, she is still in 9th grade."

Grandma: "Uh huh. Listen. I got this new iPhone, and I just don't understand how to use it. See I want to get on that Facebook… "

Teacher: "I think we should focus on your granddaughter."

Grandma: "I've been focusing on her for years. Now *I* need help."

Counselor (to a room full of teachers): "Well I guess mom isn't coming."

Teacher 1: "I'm not surprised. She hasn't returned my phone calls all year."

Teacher 2: "Me neither. She's been a no-show many times."

Counselor: "Well let's just try to call her so at least we can document that we did everything we could. *(Dials phone and puts it on speaker.)* Hello. This is your son's counselor. We were scheduled to have a meeting today."

Mom: "Yes."

Counselor: "You were supposed to meet us here for a teacher conference over an hour ago."

Mom: "Oh sorry, I'm on my period."

Counselor: "Well perhaps we can do the conference on the phone."

Mom: "No. I said I'm on my period." *(quickly hangs up)*

Counselor: "Okay, who would like to comment first?"

Mom (*pulling out phone*): "Hold on a sec, I need to facetime my husband. He couldn't make it."

Counselor: "No problem."

Mom (*holding up the phone so everyone can see her husband in bed wearing only a pair of tight underwear*): "Go ahead, honey."

Dad: "This better not be a waste of my time!"

Teacher is in the middle of a scheduled parent conference. A woman in a shower cap and slippers barges into the room and stands next to the teacher with her arms crossed.

Teacher: "Hello. I'm in a conference. Yours was scheduled for a week ago."

Shower cap: "Well I'm here now."

Teacher: "This family is here now too. And this is their scheduled time."

Shower cap: "I'll wait."

Shower cap stands over the conference until the family is so uncomfortable they decide to leave. The teacher is forced to accommodate shower cap, who wants to know why the teacher gave her kid all those zeros when she was absent.

Teacher: "I think you have the wrong classroom."

Mom: "Isn't this 150? English class?"

Teacher: "Yes, but I don't have your daughter in my class."

Dad: "I'm looking at her schedule, and it says 150."

Teacher: "May I see?"

Teacher checks name on attendance list and discovers student who has not come to class once all semester.

Teacher: "Okay. I see what the problem is. Your daughter is on my roster, but I did not recognize her name because she has never come to class before."

Dad: "What do you mean?"

Teacher: "She has never *ever* come to my class."

Mom: "But she has English homework all the time and a literature textbook. I've seen her do work in it!"

Teacher: "That's great ma'am, but she isn't doing that work for me. We don't even use a textbook."

Dad: "I guess that explains why she's failing."

Teacher: "Hello, welcome."

Dad: "I can see why my son has a crush on you. He has a thing for plus-sized women."

A father has called a conference for his kindergartener who did not get picked for an award.

Dad (*busting through the door and screaming*): "My white Lexus is stuck in the snow, and I need help getting it out *now!*"

Counselor: "Sir, we can't help you with that."

Dad: "I need help immediately! My white Lexus is stuck! I can't get it out by myself!"

Counselor: "As I said, we can't help with that. But I can call a tow truck for you."

Dad: "How dare you! This isn't the last you'll be hearing from me!"

Mom has called a conference at 6 AM (the only time she is available) to discuss her daughter's grade of 89 on the first quiz of the year.

Mom: "My daughter has *never* received a grade lower than an A."

Teacher: "That is wonderful and I understand your concern but it is the first quiz of the year, and she is only one point away from an A. I'm sure that-"

Mom: "I would like to discuss your teaching credentials. How can I view your teaching certificate? Do you have it in the building?"

Teacher: "No I don't."

Mom: "I would like you to send me a copy. How long have you been teaching?"

Teacher: "Seven years. But Mrs.-"

Mom: "I would also like you to provide me with a sample lesson so I can witness your teaching methods. All of my children attend Princeton University, and my husband is a well-known cardiologist."

Teacher: "Okay…"

Mom: "My daughter will also attend Princeton. She cannot get a B."

Teacher: "I understand, and I'm sure that if she continues with this level of effort-"

Mom: "She *cannot* get a B!"

Teacher: "Okay.

Teacher: "Your son has been very disruptive in class."

Mom: "He's really matured so much since last year. Physically I mean. I don't think he's caught up emotionally. He's still very immature. Let me show you some pictures from last year; you won't believe it!"

Teacher: "Oh that's not necessary. I know that during the summer between middle and high school some students have growth spurts."

Mom: "Yes, but he looks like he's aged ten years! Just look!"

Mom takes out phone, holds it out for the teacher to see, and begins swiping through her picture gallery. Suddenly the pictures are of different penises, about ten in a row.

Mom: "Oh I'm sure you don't want to see those! Do you?"

Teacher: "Nope!"

Mom: "Well anyway, my son just needs some time for his mental maturity to catch up to his physical maturity."

Teacher: "I'm sure that's true."

Teacher: "I am concerned that whenever we are on the computer, your son googles the words 'guns' and 'murder.'"

Dad: "I didn't know they weren't allowed to google things.

Teacher: "Your son is a fourth grader who reads on a second-grade level. I'll do everything I can to get him as close to grade level as possible, but we need your support at home."

Dad: "That's not going to happen. We're a football family, and we don't have time for that."

Parents enter the room, sit down, take out an old-school tape recorder and press record before crossing their arms and staring at the teacher.

Teacher: "Your daughter is doing well in my class. She can be very chatty, but her grades are excellent."

Mom: "Your seating chart is racist."

Teacher: "What?"

Dad: "Your seating chart is clearly racist. Our daughter was sitting in the front row, and now she is near the back. We suspect that you moved her because of her race."

Teacher: "The students pick their own seats. I moved your daughter because she would not stop talking to the girl next to her."

Mom: "Why didn't you move the other girl?"

Teacher: "She has an IEP that specifies that she must sit in the front row. Your daughter does not."

Dad: "Well why did you move her to the back row?"

Teacher: "At first I moved her one row back, but she would not stop talking there. I tried several different spots and the only one that worked was in the back row where she sits next to an empty desk."

Mom: "Racist."

Seven teachers, a counselor, and an administrator are waiting in the conference room for a meeting a mother requested as urgent.

Student: "My mom said she'd be right back she just needs to run to Starbucks."

The group waits over an hour, but the mom never came back.

"My son is very shy and has a hard time opening up. In his past life he was a llama and was killed very violently. It still affects him and his soul very deeply."

11

THINGS THAT MAKE YOU GO HMMM

"Common sense is not so common."

-Voltaire

I had a student who told me that she had tried to hang herself over the weekend. I immediately informed the administration who called her parents to pick her up. They told her parents that she would not be allowed back in the school building until she was cleared by a mental health professional. This process took two weeks. Meanwhile, the very next day one of my students took out a 10-inch long kitchen knife and threatened to slit the throats of about ten students in the class. Each student testified that this had happened but, of course, by the time they called the girl into the office she had gotten rid of the weapon. They asked her a few times if she had a knife and she said no. So they let her go back to class. The same girl continued to bring various weapons to school, but because she never had them on her when searched, there was no consequence.

So the girl who may have been a threat to herself needed to have a mental health evaluation, but the girl who threatened dozens of classmates with weapons did not?

In the words of the great Jacobim Mugatu, *"I feel like I'm taking crazy pills."*

12

INTERVIEW QUESTIONS AND WHAT THEY ARE REALLY ASKING

"Teachers hold our young people's lives in their hands. For that, they deserve more than just fond reminiscences of grateful adults. They deserve the intellectual validation, social importance, and financial security that other trained, skilled, and responsible professionals enjoy."

-Henry Louis Gates Jr

Recently I decided to try to transfer to a school that is closer to where I live. I didn't prepare much for my first interview because I had over a decade's worth of experience. The questions they asked me were jam-packed with edushit terms, and at times I couldn't even decipher what they were asking me. I bombed that first interview so hard that at one point I just started laughing. They looked at me like I was nuts. After that interview, I knew if I really wanted a shorter commute I would have to bone up on the bullshit. Here are some of the questions that showed up in my interviews and what they *really* were asking:

How do you use data to inform your teaching practices?

What they are really asking: Please throw out as many educational buzzwords as you can in the next two minutes: Ready? Go!

How I want to answer: I look at my grade book, and the kids who have grades below 60% are failing. I know that this is most likely due to a severe lack of effort on the student's part. I prepare for the onslaught of emails and phone calls from those students, their parents, and even administration requesting that the student be given every opportunity to pass, even if that means just giving them points for no reason.

How proficient are you with the latest classroom technologies?

What they are really asking: Can you use PowerPoint and Google classroom? Are you going to annoy people with dumb internet questions?

How I want to answer: I can use PowerPoint and Google Classroom. I am usually the one who gets inundated with dumb internet questions from others.

How do you handle students who are consistently tardy or absent?

What they are really asking: We have absolutely no consequences for tardies and absences so how will you make it appear that there is some kind of consequence?

How I want to answer: I will mostly ignore it, but sometimes I will get really mad and yell.

How do you differentiate for ESL students? Gifted students? Special needs

students?

What they are really asking: We are going to take kids with every possible ability level and shove them into one class. Is that okay?

How I want to answer: That sounds like a really bad idea, but it's worth a shorter commute, so whatevs.

How would you handle a situation with an "at risk" child and unreceptive parents?

What they are really asking: We have no consequences for students who are disrespectful, belligerent and out of control. If you call home, the number will most likely be disconnected, or the mom will yell at you that this is not her problem. Do you have the patience for this shit?

How I want to answer: Yes, I am on several anti-anxiety meds for this very scenario. I am armed and ready with indifference!

Describe a recent professional article or book you have read and how it informed your teaching practices.

What they are really asking: The time has come to bullshit us to the point of no mercy! Show us that you read online what an interviewer might ask you! We really get off on that sort of thing!

How I want to answer: This is obviously a joke question because if I had any extra time, I certainly wouldn't spend it reading articles written by people who have never actually been in the classroom. Next question.

What courses have you taken recently for professional development (besides those that are mandatory) and what have you learned from them?
(Note: this is the question that caused me to laugh hysterically at my first interview)

What they are really asking: Have you been desperate enough to take all those extra shitty courses for that pathetic little salary increase?

How I want to answer: It ain't worth an extra ten bucks a check. I'll make coffee at home four mornings a month instead.

How do you motivate a student who is a reluctant learner?

What they are really asking: We have lots of kids who don't give a fuck about school or life in general. Will you let them sleep in class or will you wake them up and deal with their shit?

How I want to answer: Usually I will let them sleep, for the sake of my sanity. Occasionally, when I am feeling ambitious, I will wake them up and ask them if they are going to do something. But mostly I just slip worksheets under their drooling face.

How do you use scaffolding in the classroom?

What they are really asking: Do you know what this word means? It sounds fancy, but it's really not.

How I want to answer: Yeah, I read that this means "steps." I do use steps leading up to an assignment because I'm a teacher and that's what we do.

Why do you want to work at our school specifically?

What they are really asking: Did you look at our website five minutes before this interview and memorize a few facts?

How I want to answer: I want to work here for the simple reason that it will shave 25 minutes off my commute and save me about $30 a week in gas.

Describe your classroom management style.

What they are really asking: Can you handle buck wild students yourself or are you going to be sending them to us all the time?

How I want to answer: I know not to send them to you. I try everything in my power to get them to pay attention and then I usually just give up.

What is your ideal vision for PLCs (professional learning communities)?

What they are really asking: Once or twice a week we are going to force you to meet with other teachers. How much are you going to complain about it?

How I want to answer: My ideal vision of PLCs is to go back to a time when they did not exist.

Do you have any questions for us?

What they are really asking: We would now like to judge you based on your response to this question about questions. We will give you a short, irritated answer for each of your questions.

However, if you don't ask any questions, we will be suspicious of you and wonder why you couldn't come up with a question.

How I want to answer: I wish I knew what you wanted me to ask. I know there is a perfect question, but like the holy grail of interview responses, I fear I may never discover it.

13

MY FAVORITE DAY OF THE SCHOOL YEAR

Me: "How come your friend is always in such a bad mood?"

Student: "If you were sucking dicks all day you would be in a bad mood too!"

Me: "Wow that was so inappropriate!"

Student: "What should I have said? Sucking *penises*?"

My favorite day of the school year is not what you might expect. It doesn't involve holidays, assemblies, performances or movies. The best day of the year for me is when the administrators visit the classrooms to go over the school rules. This usually occurs a few weeks into the new school year, when I have already complained about the unbelievably inappropriate and disrespectful behavior of certain students. After getting responses like, "Perhaps your lessons need to be more engaging?" and "You should observe some other teacher who is more successful in developing personal relationships with students," or simply no response at all, I relish the 45 minutes during which these administrators (who haven't been in the classroom in years) have to deal with their shit. In this particular scenario, I tried to warn the assistant principal that my class was particularly difficult. She assured me that she was particularly adept at developing relationships with students and would have no problem handling them.

The fun started early on when she began discussing school safety. Along with this is the "no hats or headgear" policy. This got the kids pretty riled up.

Admin: "For safety reasons, students may not wear hats or bandanas. The only headgear that is allowed are religious coverings."

Student 1: "Why? That's stupid!"

Admin: "Well as I said, it is for safety reasons and-"

Student 2: "How is my hat making the school unsafe?"

Admin: "During an emergency, we need to be able to identify you in security camera footage, and if you are wearing a hat it makes it difficult to do that."

Student 1: "But how does a bandana make it hard to identify me? They don't let us wear those either!"

Student 3: "Can I wear a headband?"

Student 4: "You know some people got no choice but to wear that bandana cuz they got issues with their edges!"

Admin: "Bandanas are not allowed because they are often gang-related."

Class goes apeshit…

Ten minutes later

Admin: "Next I would like to talk about fire drill procedures."

Student 5: "How come everybody always taking our phones?"

Student 6: "Yeah in the hallway they always doing too much!"

Student 1: "How come I can't use my phone in the hallway?"

Admin: "Well we haven't gotten to the cell phone policy yet, but the reason is that if you are looking down at your phone, then you are distracted and not looking where you are going."

Student 2: "That's crazy!"

Student 6: "What do you think we're like retarded or something?"

Student 4: "Yeah I just do like this…"

Student 4 gets up and demonstrates how she walks with her head down looking at her phone

Student 1: "Yeah she can still see!"

Student 4: "I never bumped into nothing!"

Admin: "Yes well I think that-"

Student 3: "And why can't we have earbuds in class? I can still hear you!"

Student 5: "Teachers are so pressed about that!"

Admin: "When we get to our discussion of cell phone pol-"

Student 7: "I heard that you take phones and keep em till Friday. That's true?"

Student 8: "They can't hold onto your shit that long!"

Student 1: "I heard that a parent has to come pick it up!"

Student 2: "But what if the student is over 18? You gonna call their parents to pick it up? 18 means you're an adult!"

Admin: "No it is not true that we hold it until Friday."

Student 8: "I told you!"

Student 2: "Okay but what if a student is 20 and they acting bad, you gonna call their parents? What if they don't got no parents?"

Admin: "If you are still here when you are 20 then we have bigger problems to deal with."

Student 2: "Whatchu mean?"

Admin: "If your behavior is that bad and you are over 18 then we will probably throw you out."

Student 2: "You can't do that! We can be here till we're 21!"

Student 9: "Why you asking? Cuz your brother was here till he was 21 and STILL didn't graduate?"

Class goes apeshit...

Ten minutes later

Admin: "Now I would like to discuss the dress code."

Student 1: "Yeah why if I'm wearing spaghetti straps that's gonna distract somebody?"

Student 2: "How come it's bad if my belly button's showing? Who cares!"

Admin: "Well basically if you are wearing something that you would not wear to a job interview then you should not wear it to school."

Student 3: "School ain't my job! I get *paid* at my job! I don't get paid *shit* to come here!"

Admin: "Alright look-"

Student 4: "I work at Bart's Deli and don't no one care if I show my belly button!"

Student 5: "That's cuz you in the back room making sandwiches by yoself!"

Student 6: "If it's hot how come I can't wear shorts?"

Admin: "You can wear shorts, but we follow the fingertip rule. Your shorts shouldn't be higher than your fingertips."

Student 8: "What if someone has really long arms? That's not fair!"

Student 2: "Yeah I can wear them short shorts cuz I got short arms!"

Student 5: "Don't nobody wanna see yo fat arms or them cottage cheese thighs!"

Student 2: "Shut the fuck up!"

Admin: "*Moving on* to the gentleman. We do not want to see your underwear hanging out."

Student 9: "But what if I got on some really nice ones like from Armani or something?"

Student 5: "You can't afford no Armani *nothing*!"

Student 2: "He can if he stole it!"

Admin: "Let's move on to-"

Student 6: "Yeah I got a question!"

Admin: "Please save your questions for-"

Student 6: "Do I gotta wear a bra?"

Admin: "Well if you're not going to, then make sure that what you are wearing adequately covers you."

Student 6: "What that means?"

Admin: "Don't wear anything sheer."

Student 6: "*Why?*"

Admin: "We shouldn't be able to see your nipples."

Class goes apeshit…

Admin: "We just have one more topic if you could please-"

Student 5: "I can't believe she said *nipples*! And you know she got them pepperoni nipples!"

Student 1: "I got a question about the bathroom!"

Admin: "Okay."

Student 1: "My teacher told me I couldn't go because I went the day before. She can do that?"

Admin: "Well if you are going too often then the teacher can limit your passes."

Student 1: "But what if I really gotta go?"

Student 2: "Yeah like if he gotta take a big nasty shit!"

Student 5: "You know she always eating that Chipotle during lunch!"

Class goes apeshit…

Admin. walks over to me looking frazzled and whispers, "I don't know how you do it."

I reply, "I don't have a choice."

She answers, "It's the worst class I've ever dealt with in my entire career. I just can't," before quickly making her escape.

I then turn to the class and exclaim, "Great work everyone!"

14

"SMELL MY SON" AND OTHER OUTRAGEOUS PARENT REQUESTS

"It is not what you do for your children, but what you teach them to do for themselves, that will make them successful human beings."

-Ann Landers

I asked my teacher followers to share their most shocking parent requests. In less than 24 hours I had over 1,000 responses. There were many who told similar stories, which I outline below.

Many parents request daily phone calls, texts and emails from the teacher, updating them about lesson plans, assignments, behavior, and grades.

Many parents still spoon feed their children in elementary school (up through 5th grade!) and expect teachers to do the same. (One even came to the school every day to spoon feed her 2nd grader during lunch. I'm sure that kid will grow up to be perfectly well adjusted.)

Many parents request that finals be moved or that their kid be allowed to take tests early or late because of a vacation. (These requests are often approved, by the way.)

Many parents expect teachers to be available to tutor their kid or meet for a conference at *any* time, including hours before school starts, during class, all hours of the night and any time on the weekend.

Many parents request that the teacher hit their kid. Some give specifics, like use a belt or slap him across the face.

Many parents request that the teacher call home on nights and weekends to help discipline their kid. Some ask the teacher to discuss specific things like cleaning their room.

Many parents request that elementary aged kids be wiped (one mom wanted a phone call when her son pooped so she could come to school and wipe him.)

I have categorized other ridiculous parent requests as such:

Bathroom concerns:

"Please warm the toilet before my child sits on it because she can't use the bathroom if the seat is cold."

A parent complained about the toilet paper in the boys' bathroom and wanted to know if the custodians could replace it with a softer kind.

A parent requested that the teacher brush their child's teeth after every meal/snack.

One mom wanted the teacher to check the color and size of her son's poop. He was a senior in high school!

A student swallowed a watch battery at home. The parent sent in a fork, clothespin, and a note asking the teacher to inspect the child's poop each time he went at school so they could find the battery.

Health concerns:

A parent asked if the teacher could keep their child from hugging or sitting too close to other children because they didn't want her to get sick.

A parent of a 1st grader asked not to have her daughter sit in line on the blacktop after recess because it would give her a yeast infection.

During an IEP[5] meeting, the parent of a 4th-grade girl requested that the teachers include a goal to address her farting in class.

A mom of a second grader sent her son to school with ringworm all over his face. She put bandages on him, but they fell off almost immediately. He scratched his face all day and then touched everything. The nurse called home, but the mom said she couldn't miss work and refused to pick him up. Of course, the other kids were curious (and grossed out) about the circles on his face and the next day she called to complain that the other kids were asking about his face. She said the teacher was at fault for allowing him to get bullied.

A parent asked the teacher to help her fourth-grade son "clean his nose out" before getting his picture taken for picture day.

A mom asked the teacher to remove a Christmas tree from the classroom because her son is allergic and that's what was causing his behavior issues. The tree was made from construction paper.

A boy would have a tantrum if staff checked on him because he was in the bathroom for too long. "Well you're going to have to teach my son to masturbate because I'm not doing it," was the father's response. For the record, the teacher was female.

A 4th-grade parent asked the teacher to track when her daughter had her period and the mood changes that came with it.

"My son is under stress when he takes assessments. Could you please squeeze his head while testing?"

"My son (in high school) needs a cot somewhere in the building because when he gets tired, we let him sleep for a little bit."

A mom wanted the teacher to set a timer for every 10 minutes to remind her daughter to drink water. When the teacher said, it would be a distraction to the rest of the class the mom said that the teacher should walk over to her privately to remind her. This was not for any medical reason; she just thought her daughter needed to drink more water.

A parent demanded her daughter be excused from disciplinary clean up (that was issued as a consequence for throwing food) because she was "allergic to trash."

A parent informed the teacher that her child would miss every day of school after a full moon due to her "full moon insomnia" and would need all assignments and tests postponed until she caught up on her sleep.

"Can you check to make sure she's wearing underwear every day?"

A parent requested that the teacher carry her 5th grader's trumpet to and from band practice because it was too heavy for him.

"Can you smell my son and tell him if he smells? I don't think he showers often. Maybe talk to him about being clean." He was 16.

A mom insisted that her son drink a cup and a half of water literally every hour. And if that kid came home and peed with even the slightest tinge of yellow in his pee, the mom went berserk!

Academic concerns:

"But you're not telling me what YOU'RE doing to help her pass your class - you keep telling me what *she* needs to do, what about *you?*" -Parent of a 10th grader

A parent wanted the teacher to tell her when her daughter handed something in late *before* it was late. She literally had to explain how time worked.

"I didn't know that doing my child's homework was going to label her a cheater."

A student had an IEP that required teachers give him a copy of the test WITH THE ANSWERS the night before so he could "study."

A parent wanted the teacher to give her a copy of her daughter's rough draft that she *hadn't* yet written. *She wanted a copy of what it should say.*

The mother of a ninth grader who was failing several classes told the teacher that it didn't matter because her son was going to be a porn star.

"She doesn't have to be smart. She has to be pretty. She will find a rich man, marry him and never use chemistry again."

"My daughter did not plagiarize because only copyrighted work can be plagiarized. She copied from a friend."

"I wrote that paper, and I thought it was pretty good! I'd like at least a B!"

"Do not give my child homework because I don't have time to help him. It's written in his IEP."

A parent wanted to see all assessments and classwork ahead of time to decide if the lessons were appropriate and to determine if her daughter could take the assessments.

"We're trying to help our 12th grader prepare for college, so we bought him a planner. We'd like *you* to fill it out and sign it every day. We're hoping he'll take well to this new responsibility."

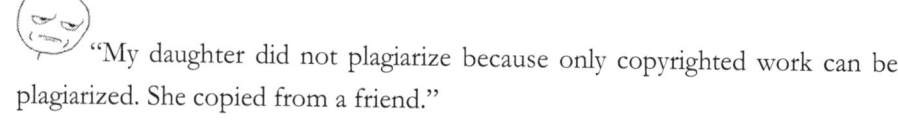

"Can you please screen my son for auditory processing disorder? I asked him to get chicken breasts out of the freezer, and he brought up chicken wings. I'm concerned."

A parent requested that a fifth grader only do half of the work that was given in class because doing all of the work gave him anxiety. She also requested that he got to pick the questions he was required to do (student has no IEP).

A mom wanted the teacher to give her son credit for the essay that he didn't write because he had done it "in his head."

"Keep a tally chart and report to me daily how many times a day you call on my daughter. She says you don't call on her enough." *The principal made the teacher do it.*

The mother of a high school freshman convinced the intervention specialist to write into her daughter's IEP that she cannot score below a 70% on any assessment or she gets a retake, regardless of the fact that she was very capable, but never did homework or studied.

A teacher was asked to teach a student in a tunnel or tent to minimize distractions.

"Call me every time my son has a failing grade because I pay too many tax dollars to check grades online."

Food concerns:

"My child can't eat the fruit from the shared fruit platter in case the parents injected drugs into them."

"Please allow my child to remain in the hallway (unsupervised) during lunch because he's vegan and can't see other children consume animals."

A mom emailed the teacher during class to ask her twins if they would rather have Taco Bell or Subway for lunch.

"Please teach my son to use his Tostitos scoops to scoop chicken salad.

"You chew the food in your mouth and then put in my son's mouth. It's called premastication."

Self-esteem concerns:

A parent asked if the teacher could put an A on all of his daughter's papers and put her real grades in the grade book. All of the D's and F's were lowering her self-esteem.

A parent demanded the teacher change her child's grade or else she would see to it that the teacher be held personally responsible for her child's low self-esteem.

In an IEP meeting, a parent asked if they could write, "teacher will frequently smile at student" as an accommodation.

A parent did not want the teacher to give Dum-Dums to her child because she thought it would hurt his self-esteem.

"Please refrain from putting an actual grade on his paper as it really hurts his feelings!"

A parent asked the teacher to change either her son's grade for the quarter or his final exam project grade. She felt the project grade should be raised since it was a group project and he had to do it by himself (because he was in in-school suspension). She felt that "summer school would hurt his spirit."

A parent emailed the teacher because her daughter had just gotten glasses.

The daughter was feeling a little self-conscious, so Mom was wondering if the teacher would set an alarm in the classroom and every 30 minutes remind the daughter how "great and beautiful" she looked in her glasses.

"I need you to motivate my son by putting inspirational quotes on a post-it and putting them on the corner of his desk every day." This is for a high school student.

A parent said that to motivate her kid the teacher would need to make sure she complimented her daily, and not just by praising her work efforts. All of her teachers needed to compliment her shoes and hair daily to encourage her to want to be in class.

Special requests:

A teacher mentioned to her class that she had attended a concert the night before. In a parent conference with the dept. chair, principal, and teacher, a parent insisted that the teacher no longer be permitted to attend weeknight concerts because she needed to, "keep her eyes on the prize of educating our country's future," like her son, who – it's worth noting- grew up to be a criminal and was incarcerated for rape.

"My husband is a teacher, and he told our son he could copy and paste from the internet as long as he changed every 3rd word because then teachers can't catch it. So it's not his fault, and you shouldn't give him a 0 for plagiarism."

Half days in a particular district used to be called "early release days," but a parent complained to the school board because "what are we releasing them from prison or something?" So now they MUST call them "early dismissal days."

A parent asked that the teacher not mention dying because she hadn't told her 6-year-old about death. It was President's Day, and they were talking about Abraham Lincoln and George Washington.

"Please email me as soon as you know you will be out sick, so I can emotionally prepare my son."

"Stop making her like art so much. I want her to be a doctor or a lawyer."

A parent of an 8th grader said that if her son couldn't sit still the teacher should let him stand beside his desk and do jumping jacks during the lesson.

Mom called to inform the teacher that her son would be bringing his knitting needles and yarn to class and that the teacher should just allow him to knit during lessons because, "unless he works all day, he's never going to finish his Christmas presents."

At the start of an IEP meeting, a parent requested that the teachers refer to her as "Sexy Chocolate."

A mom asked the teacher to give her 8th-grade son a shoulder massage whenever he got nervous.

A parent wanted the teacher to sprinkle essential oils on her daughter after lunch or when she wasn't focusing.

On the first day of school, a parent told the teacher she wanted her to keep a daily journal of everything her daughter did during the day. She wanted a detailed explanation of anything her child did wrong and what the teacher did to prevent the behavior. The student would set the book on the teacher's desk every morning and remind her to write in it.

A parent requested her child be transferred to another class because the teacher was "too fat."

A parent felt that learning about the Holocaust was too violent and requested that the teacher change the ending of the memoir *Night*.

"My son's teacher had a baby last year, and he had to have a substitute during the maternity leave so I would really appreciate it if you didn't get pregnant."

A teacher used a stop light system in kindergarten for behavior management, and a parent asked her to take it down. She was afraid her daughter would dislike the colors red, yellow and green for the rest of her life.

A parent told the principal that her very naughty child calms down if he can bounce on a trampoline for a while. She requested that the school buy a trampoline that only he could use. If he misbehaved, he could just leave and go bounce on his trampoline for half an hour.

An elementary student slapped and swore at the teacher. The mom brought in 3 huge bins of toys that only her child could play with. She told the teacher that she needed to give him more breaks throughout class to play with them. That was her solution.

A parent left a note with the office saying that her diabetic, special needs son had decided the night before that he was going to spend the weekend with his teacher, so she packed his clothes and they were in his book bag. She signed it with "Have fun!" because she was getting ready to leave town.

A dad asked the teacher to call him "Mr. Sillypants."

On the Friday before daylight savings time, the mom of a middle school girl called the school to request that no one mention anything about daylight savings time because it confused her daughter too much and gave her anxiety. They were supposed to pretend it didn't happen.

A parent called the teacher and said, "Since you're going to the school every morning anyway, can you pick up my son?"

A parent called the teacher on picture day and asked her to rub Vaseline all over her child's face before he took his picture.

The parents of an elementary student came in with a notarized (*yes, notarized*) list of demands for their child. One of the demands was that no one in the class eats gluten because they didn't want her to feel left out, even though the daughter didn't have Celiac disease. Eating gluten-free was just the family's personal choice.

Helpful Feedback:

A parent ripped into the teacher in front of the principal because he did not ask his son "the right way" to turn in his homework. Apparently "Put your homework on your desk" was mean.

A dad invited the teacher to visit his workplace because he was the CEO of a company and had 200 people under him, and the teacher could not even handle 30 kids.

A mom told a teacher who was about to go on maternity leave that it was inconsiderate to get pregnant while she was teaching her daughter, a high school senior.

A mom said it was the teacher's fault that her 8-year-old son pooped his pants because she was out sick. "He couldn't ask the sub to go to the restroom because he didn't know her."

"Your lack of experience is evident. I have clothes that are older than you."

A parent emailed the school asking if they could invest in a hawk to scare away the seagulls because one of them pooped on her son.

15

A LASTING LEGACY OF STUPIDITY

"I am patient with stupidity but not with those who are proud of it."

-Edith Sitwell

Many high schools give graduating seniors the opportunity to choose a quote to have printed underneath their picture in the yearbook. My school didn't when I was a senior, and I understand why. You are asking teenagers who are about to graduate to find some inner wisdom and maturity at a moment's notice. If you've ever spent any time around 17-year-olds, you would know that this cannot possibly go well. I'm assuming that no one edits the quotes for appropriateness or stupidity because some real gems slide though. The following is a mere sprinkling of some of the best (worst) yearbook quotes that were actually printed.

"I've been a Ho all my life." –A girl whose last name is Ho

"Being a single mom is hard especially when you are a teenage boy with no kids."

"One time I ate a bagel."

"Roses are red; violets are blue, I'm black."

"Waking up is the second hardest thing in the morning."

"My A's turned to B's and so did my grades."

"Not pregnant, just eatin' good."

"Makeup looks pretty on the outside but doesn't help if you're ugly on the inside. Unless you eat the makeup."

"That's what" –She

"In this photo, I'm not wearing pants."

"I like to eat candy."

"Money can't buy happiness but it can buy Taco Bell so that's pretty much the same thing."

"All of our parents had sex the same year so that's awesome!"

"Never hold your farts in because they travel up your spine and into your brain and that's where crappy ideas come from."

"You're laughing because I'm laughing but I'm laughing because I farted."

"I get butterflies when I think of myself!"

"I've never done cocaine but it smells good!"

"Mary had a little lamb and the doctor fainted."

"If your loved one has been diagnosed with mesothelioma you are entitled to a cash compensation."

"18 holes in one day and I still find time for golf."

"I'm fat because I don't chase these hoes."

"What if we spelled people like this- peepole. That would be funny I think."

"What if one day you woke up and you were a chicken nugget?"

"I will miss the friends I have made and the memories I share with the teachers I have boned with over the years."

"At school I learned to right good!"

"When my eyes are closed I can't see."

"Sometimes when I'm taking a bath I like to turn off the lights and pretend I'm in the womb."

"Don't drink the bong water."

"You went to high school; I went to school high."

"I'm going to end up in jail or working at the Olive Garden. Either way, endless salads will be tossed."

"When life gets hard you have to grasp it. When it comes, you have to take it on the chin. There's no such thing as getting off easy."

"In the future, I would like to find an old man, wait for him to die, and take all his money."

"My mom should have swallowed me."

16

SORRY FOR THE INCONTINENCE:

REAL NOTES AND EMAILS

"Can y'all stop being on my dick?"

-Parent response to a message

about his child's excessive absences

I consider myself very fortunate to be the recipient of copies of outrageous emails and letters that teachers all over the country have received. Each one confirms the fact that the level of respect that teachers get is about as low as it can go. Parents and students no longer have to say how they feel to a teacher's face. They merely pound it into their keyboard, press send, and move on with their stupid day. But those emails exist forever, and I am happy to be the one to shed light on this entertaining yet disturbing lack of respect.

I cannot stress enough that these are 100% real.

As we see in this first email from a student, sometimes merely a word will suffice. I must applaud the student for including "respectfully." That makes up for the stupid content of the email.

In this handwritten letter, a grandparent accuses a teacher of stealing pencils from her son (who is also her grandson- try to work that one out). If I could answer this one I would say, "Listen lady, if the cops don't care that my kids sell weed in class, they probably won't be too concerned about the fact that I 'stold' your son/grandson's pencils."

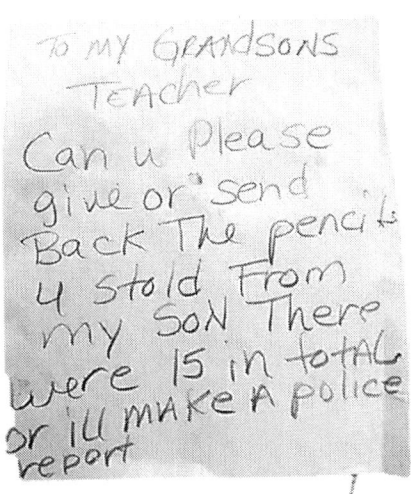

In this next baffling email, a mom hopes the teacher had a wonderful weekend but is also speaking on behalf of other mothers about what should and should not be happening in class! And she uses a lot of exclamation points because she is really looking forward to hearing back!!!!!!!!!!

Hi! Hope you had a wonderful weekend! I just wanted to let you know that I am having a little trouble understanding what you do in your classroom along with some other mothers! First, Aidan is in a co taught class! Which I was unaware of but glad! There should be no way a student should be failing with having two teachers! Second, you should be teaching and working on these assignments during their hour with you! Then if they did not finish that should be done at home! Last, how are they studying for the quizzes! This last one was extremely hard! We had to google each one and took forever! It should not be this hard!!!!!! Looking forward to hearing from you!

*After the teacher was out for a week, a student sent the following email. It was **not** sent anonymously.*

To: Ms. ▉▉▉▉   Hide

No Subject
Today at 9:24 AM

sup baby where you at i miss that ass of yours

This next artifact is not an email, but a discipline referral that is very fun to read if you do not need to be in this classroom on a daily basis.

Category	Reason	St
Disruption/Disrespect	██████████████struggles to control his flatulence in the classroom. To the extent that he roams the classroom intentionally releasing his digestive fumes within close proximity to other students for the purpose of disturbing them. Today [████] even went to the extent to ( ) release his gases on the teacher. A meeting should be held with a parent/guardian to discuss this truly disturbing behavior as it has caused whole class disturbances in all of his classes, and is a concern of his teachers and peers.	Res

In the following email, a mother responds to her daughter's teacher about allegations that her daughter was stealing. It was the third time this child had stolen something from another student, hidden the item and lied about it. The same student, at 8 years old, feels comfortable calling out, "I hate the teacher!" in the middle of class.

I don't care what my daughter did !!!
You do not get to yell at her and tell
her that you are mad or talk to her the
way you did !!!!!!! I want my daughter
transferred out of your class
immediately ! You are not her mother
or anyone in a place to raise your
voice at her " cause you're mad" thats
why I'm her mother !!!!! I get discipline
her if I need to ! I cannot Believe that
you treated my daughter that way !!!!
You're an ignorant teacher ! If anyone
should know better it should be you
since you chose to be a teacher and
deal with children ! How to I explain to
my kid that is asking me " why is the
teacher yelling at me Mommy?" How
do I explain to her that you are probably insane thinking you can scream at
my kid cause you are "mad" You don't
yell at someone else's child specially
if you are suppose to be the example
to them !!!! Smh! This is unbelievable !
Just mind blowing !

In this next email, a teacher gets reprimanded for calling a student "kiddo."

I would appreciate if you don't call my kid kiddo.
So much for professional..

This is an email a teacher had to send to a parent to document a student's behavior. The mother never responded.

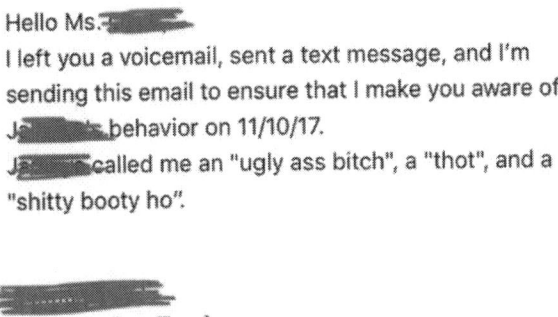

Hello Ms. ▓▓▓
I left you a voicemail, sent a text message, and I'm sending this email to ensure that I make you aware of J▓▓▓ behavior on 11/10/17.
J▓▓▓ called me an "ugly ass bitch", a "thot", and a "shitty booty ho".

▓▓▓▓▓
Language Arts Teacher

*In the following remarkable email, a student sent four simple words to **all** of his teachers.*

Student Message From ▓ ▓n
To: ▓▓▓
Reply-To: ▓▓▓

fuck all of you

I consider the following parent email to be the most extraordinary correspondence I have ever been privy to. The mother was extremely upset that the teacher put a zero into the grade book for an assignment that her daughter never turned in.

Teacher,

This is a cease and desist.

Remove immediately the 0 you gaved my child and correctly grade her for her efforts.

Where did you get your teaching certificate.

where did you get your life skills training, on giving students FAVOR and helping them to succeed. Who hired you as a teacher to most precious children, was this an E HIRED.

You have traumatic.

Never in all my life have I heard a child get a zero. Birth certificate has a number

At mc Donald's has a number, even to give confession to the Priest you have a number. We all have social security numbers

Zero means exactly that.

This is an abomination of Catastrophic proportions,

how dare you, how dare you.

███████ is not perfect as a teacher you are supposed to build and encouraged, this even sounded RACIST.

I have never met you, just assuming.

Your Zero sounds like what Martin Luther king Talked about.

Shame on you Ms ███████

This email is equal parts cute, sad and funny. Kudos to the parents for advocating for their child and being respectful at the same time. Imagine that!

Hello Ms. XXX

This is XXXXX mother. He will not be attending school on March 17th 2016 because Tuesday and Wednesday he peed his pants during school and is constantly saying that he's "afraid that leprechauns will show up at school". If you can please keep an eye on him on Friday because we aren't sure if he's had these accidents because he's really scared of leprechauns. Please let me know of anything you see thank you so much, we appreciate everything you do and I apologize you have to do all of this for us but we are super worried.

This email is from a mother who felt the need to give a detailed introduction about her daughter at the beginning of the school year. Most of the information serves no purpose other than making the teacher uncomfortable.

She was such an easy-going baby that I felt ~~my happy when I took~~ her. I breastfed her until she was 33 months old, and she still remembers the taste of my breastmilk-she says it was so sweet and had some nutty flavour. It's really amazing that she can still ~~recall the moment (In fact, I'm a breastfeeding~~ consultant, and I'm pleased to see what I have learnt is true).

We go to the Catholic church on every Sunday.

Teachers often receive emails from former students that reveal their true feelings. The students do not bother to send such emails anonymously because they know that there are no consequences for this type of behavior.

Dear ugly,
You are the worst imaginable teacher in the history of the past five years of ~~████~~ ~~████~~. I hope you get fired from your job and never get to expierience a date with ~~████~~ A.K.A ██ and btw your Instagram is about as famous as my left nut.

In this next gem, a parent expresses her frustration with the school system and English curriculum. She makes some viable points at first, but things start to get a little strange after that.

What is it that you want ~~████~~ to know in your English classes as of right now, I wonder?
Please don't tell me William Shakespeare's mind.   That mans head was always in the clouds.   Let all that be taught in colleges I say. There's artists who need those writing skills because they want a shot in the dark to become a play writer too.
Have mercy on me!!! The boy just wants to mechanic and own his own trucks and make a business out of that. Not fairy tales. LOL. GIVE ME A BREAK ONE WORLD ORDER TEACHING PROGRAM. WHO DO I BLAME HERE? I don't know. Lol.

This type of email comes from the parent of a special snowflake. Her daughter is bored and needs an enrichment class that will offer trophies and medals. This is not too much to ask!

solicitation)

6 hrs ·

Is there any place that offers academic enrichment for grade schoolers? My daughter is getting bored in school, she needs more of a challenge. I am not looking for a kumon style class. I really want something that offers trophies or medals for outstanding effort and outcome. Does this exist?

This extraordinary young man somehow believes that his teacher is not only going to give him a passing grade for no reason but should also give him an A. Dream big kid!

To You, + 1   ○ ○ ○

do you think you can raise my grade up to a passing grade and i'll come to your class prepared and ready to learn wont get on my phone and ill go on time everyday please raise my grade to a B or A

This is a correspondence that is automatically sent to parents when their child is late or absent from a class along with a father's classy response.

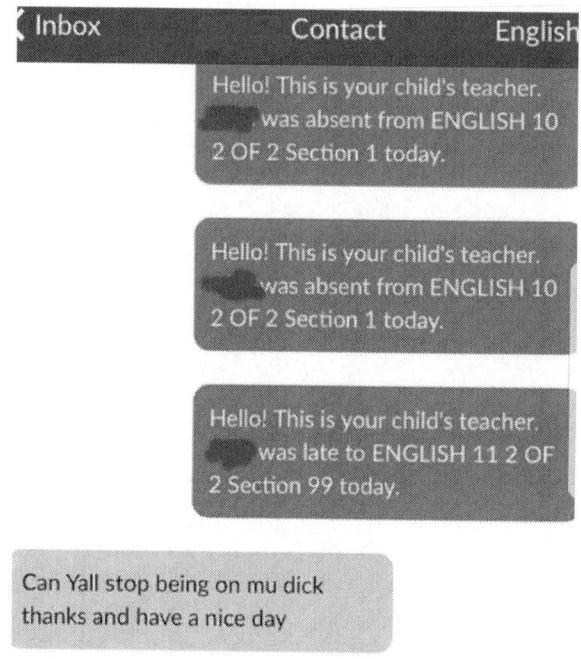

Hello! This is your child's teacher. _____ was absent from ENGLISH 10 2 OF 2 Section 1 today.

Hello! This is your child's teacher. _____ was absent from ENGLISH 10 2 OF 2 Section 1 today.

Hello! This is your child's teacher. _____ was late to ENGLISH 11 2 OF 2 Section 99 today.

Can Yall stop being on mu dick thanks and have a nice day

A kindergarten teacher asked that every parent pack extra layers of clothing so their kids wouldn't be cold during early morning recess. This is a mother's response:

hi chelsea can you please be sure to worry about teaching my daughter what she need to learn in kindergarten and not about what she wants to wear thanks.

This parent has a simple request. Please email or text her son's grades because she does not have the free time to look online for herself.

> No problem. Thank you for letting me know about his grades. I know canvases there for parents to access whenever they have free time but honestly I don't have

> free time. Corresponding through emails or text messages it's so much easier for me then getting on the computer and looking.

Non-teachers have a hard time believing that the next email is real. Knowing the context helps to suspend that disbelief. The email was sent from a mother who was admittedly in Las Vegas on vacation. Note that it was sent at 4:57 AM. When the school contacted her about the email, she claimed that her email was hacked. Yet, the hacker somehow knew her son's name.

To:  M ▬▬▬▬▬▬

Date: October 1, 2015, 4:57 AM

You listen here buddy, if I find out what little ▬▬▬▬ says is true and you actually took a shit in his backpack I will fuck you up, I shit you not .

-Concerned Parent

This well-intentioned message comes from a mother who does not quite agree with some of the teacher's policies. But she softens her approach by adding the beauty of prayer.

I would like to start off by saying how disappointed I am of your grading scale. How can you give a student a failing grade when he did his assignment? Did you take into account he did everything you asked and you even assigned a paper during Spring break? So dumb. ▮▮▮ went to the VU library and got books and quoted sites, he searched the Internet and quoted sites, he quoted from the Bible and wrote note cards and did his title page and outline like you asked. He printed 2 copies like you asked and he turned it in on time but yet you still fail him? How dare you! I hope you sleep good at night and God says to pray for the wicked and cold hearted. So I am praying for you. Please don't respond because teachers like you don't deserve a parents time!

The next memo was sent from a parent who can't understand why the school isn't raising her child for her. Is that really so much to ask? Besides, it's only junior high school. Nothing that happens there actually matters.

And i can not force her to attend PE if she is cutting that is an issue you should take up with her counselor Ms. ████/your AP or your principal I dont understand how she can cut class n still be in school .On my end all I can do is tell her but i believe it's the schools responsibility it is only JHS

This message was sent from what seems to be the most arrogant, rude, entitled little shit the world has ever known. It still blows my mind that she thinks offending someone will help get her what she wants.

RS ████████   May 21
To You   •••

Sorry to interrupt your incredibly busy busy night of not grading assignments, but I was just informed that I have an F in your class.

Whoopdie doo, now I'm on academic probation on Tuesday and Wednesday which happen to be days that I'm scheduled to WORK on. You know, where you have a job and do it.

I know for a fact that I completed and turned in both assignments that you listed as missing. This was the last thing I needed right now.

Not happy. Please fix it ASAP.

This is an email sent from a teacher to a student and the student's response. I love the simplicity of the student's message. It gets straight to the point. Also, the detention is only 20 minutes? For real?

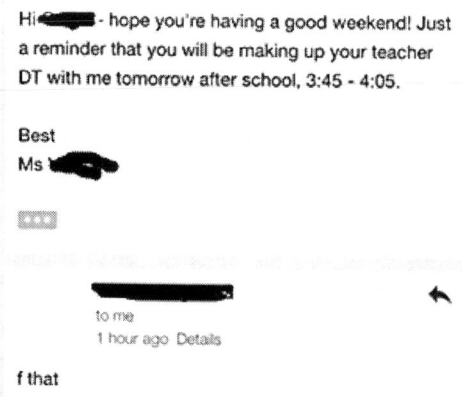

Remember a few emails ago when I commented that a student was the most arrogant, rude, entitled little shit the world has ever known? Well, this next email really gives her some stiff competition! Let's just hope these two don't procreate! Imagine what THAT kid would be like!

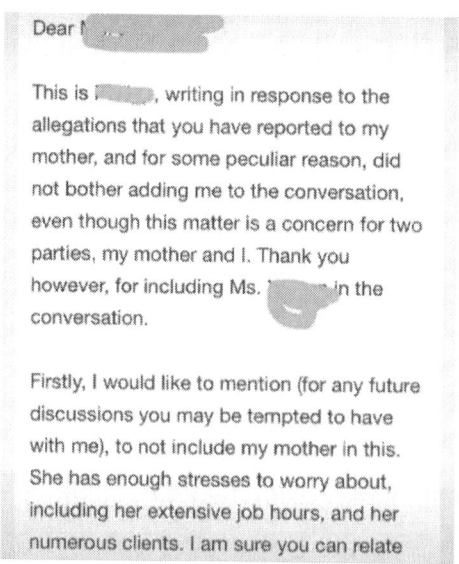

with me), to not include my mother in this. She has enough stresses to worry about, including her extensive job hours, and her numerous clients. I am sure you can relate to this, and hopefully understand, as her well-being is important to me.

Secondly, I do not participate in ample classroom discussions due to a condition I currently possess, which voids me from participating in any lengthy verbal communications, especially in a classroom environment which can be stressful for me. If you have any further questions regarding this, I would be more than content to answer them for you tomorrow, or at any other available date.

Thank you for your ongoing contribution, and your agility communicating your concerns. I feel more than confident that I made myself clear to you.

If you have any future dilemmas you would like addressed, please be sure to **include my address** in the discussion, and **only in the worst situations,** have my mother involved.

This student somehow got the idea that being a dick in an email would help improve her grades.

Good morning mrs ■■■■. i understand your decision on how everyone who plagiarized gets a zero. But i would like to know the logic behind you literally waiting till the day the quarter closes to put in zeros for more than half of the students that take your class and bring them down TWO whole letter grades, not giving any of us time to bring up our grade or not giving us any warning that we SHOULD do both the extra credits, that is what is really confusing me. I don't know what's going on in your personal life but that should never affect your students and you should NEVER take that out on us. Don't get mad at me for using my voice because this whole situation is SO messed up. Let me know lol.
Thanks

Okay, prepare yourself for the biggest load of helicopter parent horseshit you've ever read…

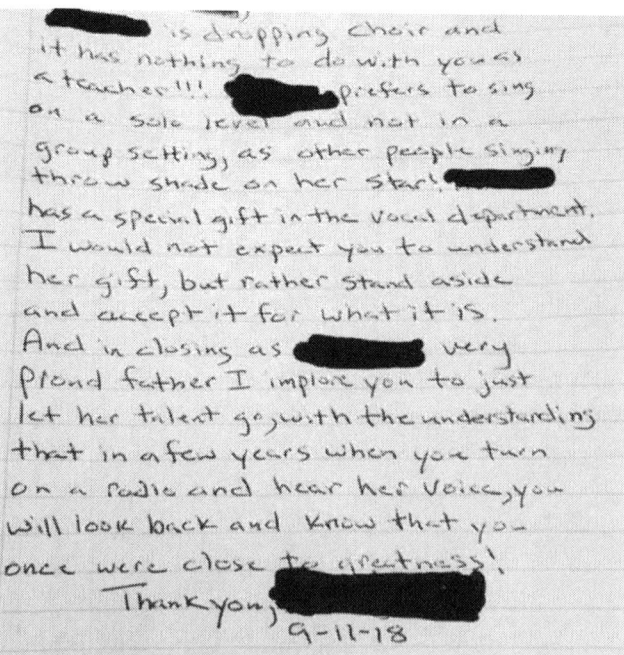

■■■■ is dropping choir and it has nothing to do with you as a teacher!!! ■■■■ prefers to sing on a solo level and not in a group setting, as other people singing throw shade on her star! ■■■■ has a special gift in the vocal department. I would not expect you to understand her gift, but rather stand aside and accept it for what it is. And in closing as ■■■■ very proud father I implore you to just let her talent go, with the understanding that in a few years when you turn on a radio and hear her voice, you will look back and know that you once were close to greatness! Thank you, ■■■■ 9-11-18

Hello,

I am emailing you to let you know that
I will not be at school tomorrow
because of something that has come
up. If there is any work that I need to do
please feel free to email me what it is or
what I will miss. I don't know when I will
be back. I'm sorry for the incontinence.

Sigh.

SEPARATION OF CHURCH, STATE, AND GRIZZLIES

"I hesitate to talk about all schools in general because schools are made up of individual students attending them."

-U.S. Secretary of Education

Betsy DeVos

Note: This chapter is dense and not all that funny. But it is really important. So if you're just here for the laughs, and a quick bit of insight, the most significant points are in bold. Also, let me say that I do not find this political. It really isn't about parties. It's about picking someone who best serves the nation's students and teachers, and not who chose them.

Just when the teaching profession couldn't get any shittier, a Secretary of Education with zero experience in education is elected. Billionaire Betsy DeVos does not hold any degrees in education, has never taught a class or been an administrator. Until she took this position, she had never even stepped inside a public school. DeVos earned a bachelor's degree in business economics in 1979 from Calvin College, a private Christian liberal arts college. Before her nomination, 2,700 Calvin students and alumni protested her nomination as Education Secretary in an open letter where they discussed her lack of experience.[6] Senate offices received more calls opposing DeVos than any other Cabinet nominee. And now that she is in office, she faces so many protests at public appearances that she receives special protection from the U.S. Marshals Service, at an average cost of $1 million a month.[7] *So why does everyone hate her so much?*

DeVos only went to private Christian schools and sent her kids to private Christian schools. As I mentioned, she has *never* worked in education, public or private. She is very committed to private religious schools and donates to them. On the first day of her confirmation hearing, DeVos indicated a lack of support for federal policies regarding educational systems that receive public funding. This is especially concerning given that the Individuals with Disabilities Education Act and Title IX, which ensure that all students' educational experiences are free of discrimination that impedes learning, are not of value to her.

Looking into this woman's past is a long, complicated journey. But it is an important one since **she now controls the country's $1 trillion student loan**

bank. So let me break it down for you as best I can.

Betsy is the daughter of Edgar Prince, who founded a manufacturing company worth more than $1 billion. Betsy's husband Dick is the eldest son of the co-founder of Amway, a multinational corporation with $9.5 billion. Together, Betsy and Dick are worth $5 billion. Both were raised in strictly Christian households. **One of the main beliefs of the DeVos' is that there should *not* be a separation of church and state.** Dick once wrote, "The real strength of America is its religious tradition. This country was built on a religious heritage, and we'd better get back to it. We must help America become as it was when first founded- a Christian Republic."[8] **In order to make America more of a Christian republic, the DeVos' main weapon is public education.**

In 2001, Betsy spoke at "The Gathering," an annual meeting of some of America's wealthiest Christians. She explained the reasoning behind her arduous fight for education reform with Biblical allusions. "It goes back to the concept of really being active in the Shephelah[9] of our culture- to impact our culture in ways that are not the traditional route, but that really may have greater kingdom gain in the long run by changing the way we approach things- in this case, the system of education in the country."[10] Her husband added, "The church- which ought to be far more central to the life of the community- has been displaced by the public school. We can think of no better way to rebuild our communities than to have that circle of church and school much more tightly focused." Even if you're a devout Christian, if you live in America you should be alarmed by those statements. One of the reasons America was founded was to keep church and state separate. AND THESE TWO WANT CHURCH AND SCHOOL TO BE THE SAME THING, FOR EVERYONE.

To accomplish their goal of getting public funding for private religious schools, the DeVos' created the Great Lakes Education Project (GLEP). This organization had a singular focus: education reform.[11] In 2002, GLEP had more money than the Michigan Education Association. Dick and Betsy[12] pushed hard for a constitutional amendment that would siphon funds from public schools to private schools, but they were unsuccessful. Yet their efforts still completely changed the educational system in Michigan. There is no cap on the number of charter schools, and there is *no public oversight of charter schools*. About 80 percent of Michigan's 300 publicly funded charter schools are operated by for-profit companies. Basically, tax dollars that would otherwise go to public schools are used to buy supplies that become private property.[13] Though a charter school is not supposed to be religiously affiliated, many find ways around it, like hiring a priest as head of the school board or having school inside a church. **The most important thing to note about charter schools is that "they perform below the state's averages on tests."**[14] Essentially, this debate means nothing if students at charter schools do not perform any better than public school students.

Another important aspect of DeVos' background is that **she invests in a number of firms that have found ways to profit off of public education, such as** *a student loan debt collection company.* Yeah, you read that right. "Among them is LMF WF Portfolio, a company which helped finance a $147 million loan to a debt collection agency that does business with the Department of Education, called Performant Financial. After receiving a flood of complaints about abusive collection practices, the Consumer Finance Protection Bureau is considering further regulating the debt collection industry and proposed new rules in 2016."[15] This is something that DeVos could directly influence. **So basically DeVos owns part of a student debt collection agency that is known for abusive practices, and now has the power to block regulations designed to prevent such abuses. Cool.**

Now DeVos, a tireless advocate of publicly funded private Christian education, partial owner of a student debt collection firm and **possessor of the kind of face you want to slap**, is head of the largest public education agency in the country. She is the first head of the education department in 30 years without any experience in government, school administration or teaching. The Secretary of Education is responsible for controlling a $1 trillion student loan bank and dealing out $30 billion in grants to students every year. The financial futures of an entire generation of people depend on this person. Yet she has no direct experience in running a bank, has never overseen a loan program of any kind, or even borrowed from one. **And she refused to commit to enforcing federal rules that prevent waste, fraud, and abuse** against predatory for-profit institutions like the ITT Technical Institutes which were shut down by the previous administration.[16]

All DeVos really cares about is her stupid voucher program. Other than vouchers, Betsy doesn't know or care about anything else in education. So let's take a quick look at this idea of vouchers. States offer school voucher programs as a way to give parents choice in which school their child attends. Parents can receive *some* public education funds to use toward the cost of private school. Yes, the idea that parents from any economic background could choose what schools their kids attend, including private schools, is great. However, this voucher idea ain't all it's cracked up to be. First of all, **the funding is removed from the public schools and given to the private schools.**[17] Even if you have a voucher, a private school doesn't have to admit your child as a public school does. And after admittance, they can expel your child for any reason. **Private schools can set their own policies for enrollment and discipline.** This is dangerous because, without any regulation on admission, discrimination can happen easily. During her confirmation hearing, DeVos was asked if the federal government would bar funding for private schools that discriminate. She said states would be required to "set up the rules around that," which meant she would not (or could not) answer this simple question. Besides having no regulations or policies on admission, **there really isn't any oversight on anything in private schools at all.** The Individuals with Disabilities Education Act does not apply to private schools. If a student needs an evaluation, or any kind of therapy such as speech or occupational, the school does not have to provide it and will, most likely, charge extra for it. **Private schools don't need to be accredited or follow any guidance about curriculum.** "There are several instances of private schools fudging health and safety records, and hiring staff with criminal backgrounds."[18] Charter schools have prompted a for-profit management industry that cares more about making money than educating children.

People will say that this gives lower-income families the choice of a better education. When in fact, "**Vouchers do little to help the poor.** The payments often do not cover the entire cost of tuition or other mandatory fees for private schools. Thus, only families with the money to cover the cost of the rest of the tuition, uniforms, transportation, books and other supplies benefit from the vouchers. In Cleveland, the majority of families who were granted a voucher cited the additional costs as the reason they could not use the voucher. Vouchers actually hurt low-income families by undermining the public schools they rely on."[19] The programs that would be cut to fund vouchers are vital to our public schools. **DeVos wants to cut funding for after-school programs and a grant program that helps low-income students go to college. She also wanted to ax grants for mental-health programs.**[20] Given the recent explosion of school shootings, we certainly cannot afford to lose mental health grants.

Only a few weeks into her new position and DeVos was already showing her incompetence. She said East Hartford High School is "nothing more than adult day care, a dangerous daycare," based on the story of one student named Michael. "Teachers sent a message that they didn't think Michael would amount to much," Betsy declared. She did absolutely no research on this school but made this extremely insulting comment nonetheless. DeVos visited a middle school in Washington D.C. and later said the teachers she met were in "receive mode" and are "waiting to be told what they have to do," rather than "empowered to facilitate great teaching." The school, Jefferson Academy, replied with, "If you mean we 'receive' students at a 2nd-grade level and move them to an 8th-grade level." **One visit to a school and she threw all the teachers under the bus.**

Next, DeVos showed how little she knows about history when she wrote, "HBCUs (historically black colleges and universities) are real pioneers when it comes to school choice. They are living proof that when more options are provided to students, they are afforded greater access and greater quality." **She seemed to have forgotten about Jim Crow laws and racist policies that would not *allow* black students to attend any other universities.**

Perhaps her most entertaining remark so far has been her comment on whether guns should be allowed on school campuses. **She said that a certain Wyoming school might need a firearm "to protect from potential grizzlies."** Everyone laughed and waited for a real answer, but all she said was the same answer she gives for almost any question she is asked, "It's best left up to the states." Then she closed with this remark, "But senator, if the question is around gun violence and the results of that, please know that I, I — my heart

130

bleeds and is broken for those families that have lost any individual due to gun violence."[21]

On July 6, 2017 attorneys general from 18 states and Washington, D.C. filed a complaint against DeVos and the Education Department "for halting the Borrower Defense Rule, which erases federal student loan debt for students cheated by for-profit colleges."[22] According to Massachusetts Attorney General Maura Healey, "Since Day 1, **Secretary DeVos has sided with for-profit school executives against students and families drowning in unaffordable student loans.**"[23] Changes to the rule simplifying the claims process for defrauded borrowers were set to take effect on July, 1, however, DeVos unilaterally suspended the changes.[24]

On June 20, 2017, she announced her plans to appoint Arthur Wayne Johnson as the Chief Operating Office Federal Student Aid (FSA). Johnson is currently the chief executive officer and director of a private student loan company, which obviously raises possible conflicts of interest and ethical concerns. Of course, his association with the company was not included in the press release issued by the Department of Education. U.S. Senator Patty Murray of Washington told the Washington Post that she had "major concerns about a private student loan CEO in such a critical position and will be examining his background closely and following up with questions about potential conflicts of interest and ethical issues."[25] Johnson has been a beneficiary of corporate profits stemming from collecting student loan debts, and it remains unclear whether or not he will advocate for college students' rights as the head of the FSA.

DeVos reinstated hefty collection fees for borrowers who have defaulted[26] and started to take apart two major consumer protection rules. One of the rules holds non-degree career education programs accountable when graduates have too much debt; the other is on borrower defense, which allows student borrowers defrauded by institutions to get loan forgiveness.[27] According to Senator Patty Murray, "**Hundreds of thousands of students were defrauded and cheated by predatory colleges that broke the law, but today's report confirms Secretary DeVos tried to shirk her responsibility to these students and shut down the borrower-defense program,** leaving them with nowhere to turn."[28] *Well, ain't that just dandy?*

What does it say about a country's educational system when a person who has never taught a day in her life, never studied educational history, theory or methods and hadn't even stepped foot inside a public school, gets to make major decisions that impact an entire nation of kids and young adults? It tells you that the country's educational system is seriously effed up, and **people need to wake up and fix it!** And they can begin by asking actual teachers, the ones who do the job every day, where to start.

18

ANYONE CAN BE A PARENT, SERIOUSLY, *ANYONE*

"I'm gonna name my kids after my favorite cartoon,
Transformers. That'd be great!
'Optimus Prime come here for a second,
I wanna talk to you.
You sit next to Megatron;
We're gonna have a little
chit-chat over here.' "

-Dane Cook

The government requires you to obtain a license to drive, own a gun, fish, hunt, teach, practice law, practice medicine, fly a plane, sell alcohol, get married and to operate a forklift. Some lesser known things that require a license are breeding dogs, babysitting, having a garage sale, performing in public, building a garage, opening a lemonade stand, becoming a tour guide, or selling raw milk, Christmas trees, and pumpkins (in some places). But create and have complete control over a human being? Open to anyone![1]

Imagine choosing a name for your newborn child that is so outrageous, mean or stupid that the authorities have to intervene? Here is a list of names that people around the world tried to assign to their baby, only to be rejected by the government:

Martian, Smelly Head, Rogue, Monkey, Devil, Dickhead, LOL, Batman, Ikea, Snort, Circumcision, Spinach (requested 3 separate times), *, Talula Does The Hula From Hawaii, 4Real, Anal, 89, Metallica, Superman, Mafia No Fear, Cyanide, Brfxxccxxmnpcccclllmmnprxvclmnckssqlbb11116, Q, Peniskin (requested 6 separate times), Terminator, Rolling Stone, James Bond, Christmas Day, Burger King,[29] Nutella, Anus, Pluto, Snake, Sexual Intercourse, Hunchback, Insane, Facebook, Rambo, Fat Boy,[30] Robocop, @, Scrotum, Fish and Chips, Bridge, Light Breeze, Devil, Viagra, Google, Lego, and (my personal favorite) Sex Fruit.

However, the following names were totally cool with governments around our globe: Gennah Tyles (think about that one for a minute), Like, Midnight Chardonnay, Number 16 Bus Shelter, Violence, Little Sweet Meat, Orgasm, Melanomia, L'Oreal, DKNY, Abstinence, Olive Garden, Ssst, Rage, Peyote, Hashtag, Xerox, Sadman, Laxative, Flora Toilet, Fishy Scales, Leper, and Hairy Berry.

Yes, that's right. *Anyone* can have kids.

---

[1] I'm not necessarily saying it *should* require a license because I've read enough dystopian novels to be wary of that.

19

WHY I SHOULD HAVE BECOME A GARBAGE WOMAN

"June is a strange month for teachers because they go from
being academic leaders- from shaping the minds and morals of
future citizens and being filled with purpose- to serving
cocktails, painting houses, and
selling flat screens at Best Buy."

-Dave Eggers

It's hard to get accurate numbers on teaching salaries in America. Data for each state is published by many different agencies and organizations every year, and none of it is exactly the same. In the same year, you may see one source claim that South Dakota has the lowest teacher pay, yet another story may say Arizona is the worst. To get an accurate picture, I asked my teacher followers for the number of years they have been teaching, their yearly salary and what state they live in. I took information for each state that seemed to match with what most others in that state were making, given the amount of experience. Yes, in some places the cost of living is much higher, and that is why those teachers make more and vice versa. But I think we can all agree that no matter where you live, 35K is not enough money to live comfortably, especially for someone with an advanced degree. And for those that live in the costliest places, such as D.C., New York City or San Diego, even 60K is definitely not enough to comfortably support a family.

Keep in mind that all of these teachers have at least one master's degree. Also remember that the average student loan payment for these teachers is 50K[31], though for some it is much higher.

Alabama- 15 yrs. experience, 49K

Alaska- 5 yrs. experience, 40K

Arizona- 18 yrs. experience, 35K

Arkansas- 9 yrs. experience, 35K

California- 8 yrs. experience, 50K

Colorado- 9 yrs. experience, holds a Ph.D., 64K

Connecticut- 9 yrs. experience, 61K

D.C.- 10 yrs. experience, 60K

Delaware- 15 yrs. experience, 48K

Florida- 10 yrs. experience, 47K

Georgia- 13 yrs. experience, 41K
 32 yrs. experience, 69K

Hawaii- 12 yrs. experience, 52K

Idaho- 17 yrs. experience, 54K

Illinois (Chicago)- 9 yrs. experience- 60K (pays $800 a month for insurance)

8 yrs. experience, 37K (9.4% goes to retirement)

Indiana- 10 yrs. experience, 42K

Iowa- 11 yrs. experience, 60K

Kansas- 8 yrs. experience, 36K

Kentucky- 5 yrs. experience, 42K

Louisiana- 4 yrs. experience, 40K

Maine- 11 yrs. experience, 51K

Maryland- 9 yrs. experience, 54K

Massachusetts- 3 yrs. experience, 52K

Michigan- 4 yrs. experience, 36K

Minnesota- 5 yrs. experience, 55K

Mississippi- 11 yrs. experience, 43K

Missouri- 19 yrs. experience, 30K

Montana- 12 yrs. experience, 51

Nebraska- 13 yrs. experience, 52K

Nevada- 6 yrs. experience, 36K

New Hampshire- 4 yrs. experience, 46K

New Jersey- 10 yrs. experience, 63K

New Mexico- 10 yrs. experience, 28K

New York- 7 yrs. experience in NYC, 2 masters degrees, 62K

For comparison, the average salary for a sanitation worker in N.Y. is $69,339 with 6 years' experience, not including holiday and overtime pay. With the extras thrown in, veteran sanitation workers average more than $80,000 a year and enjoy full pension and health benefits. One only needs a high school diploma to qualify, which means they have no student loan debt.[32] I know some people might say that sanitation work is difficult physical labor which most people would not want to do. But I am not joking when I say that handling garbage just might be preferable to being treated like garbage on a daily basis. For example, today I asked a student to put her phone away, and she told me to "fuck off." When I called her mom, she defended her daughter with, "Well she don't like you." When I wrote her up for this, the assistant principal responded that they are having a parent conference later that month. (There will be no consequence.) This is a normal occurrence for me. So yes, it might be nicer to handle people's trash for a higher salary, than to be treated like trash.

North Carolina- 5 yrs. experience, 47K

North Dakota- 12 yrs. experience, 46K

Ohio- 4 yrs. experience, 40K

Oklahoma- 19 yrs. experience, 43K

Oregon- 5 yrs. experience, 43K

Pennsylvania- 14 yrs. experience, 57K

Rhode Island- 8 yrs. experience, 66K

South Carolina- 3 yrs. experience, after taxes 23K

South Dakota- 4 yrs. experience, 39K

Tennessee- 15 yrs. experience, 45K

Texas- yrs. experience, 45K

Utah- 9 yrs. experience, 45k

Vermont- 8 yrs. experience, 51k

Virginia- *holds 2 masters degrees*, 16 yrs. experience, 69K

(This teacher shared that in this very expensive part of Virginia, childcare costs $2600 a month)

15 yrs. experience, *43K (with a 4K deductible for insurance)*

Washington- 17 yrs. experience, holds Ph.D., 68K

West Virginia- 11 yrs. experience, 42K

Wisconsin- 9 yrs. experience, 50k

Wyoming- 11 yrs. experience, 45k

Now compare those teacher salaries with the following:

Postal workers, rail track laying equipment operators, brick laying masons, earth drillers, costume attendants in theatres, crane operators, and steel workers have an average salary across the U.S. of $51K. They only need a high school education.[33]

Other jobs that on average pay better than teaching (and require only a high school diploma):

Drivers' licensing examiners- 69K

Casino managers- 78K

Customs inspectors- 80K

Elevator repair workers- 80K

When you explain these points to people, many of them will say that teachers have always been paid poorly and people shouldn't become teachers if they do not accept that. I have to call major bullshit on that one. If people avoided the career of teaching because of the pay, we would have very few teachers left. Just because that's the way it is, *does not make it acceptable*. We're not asking to be rich; we just want to comfortably support ourselves and our families without getting a second or third job. We're educators, not nuns. We shouldn't have to take a vow of poverty because we want to teach.

I asked my teacher followers what other jobs they take on during the summer and also throughout the school year. Here were some of the responses:

In the summer many teachers can be found working at a summer camp. This might not sound so bad if you've ever been a camper, but I did this for many years and trust me, you are worked to the bone for an obscenely low amount of money. A summer camp counselor's hourly salary ranges from $6 to $12 nationally, and that's before taxes.[34] If they teach lessons, such as swimming or art, the pay isn't usually much more than what a counselor makes.

Of course, many teachers also teach summer school. In my district (and many others I'm sure) it used to be that they couldn't find teachers who were willing to teach summer school. I'm sure you can imagine why. Now teachers are in such a desperate financial situation that there is a huge waiting list to teach summer school. They choose candidates by seniority, and many teachers do not get a placement and are told to try again the following year. Imagine being turned away from spending an additional 4-6 hours a day on top of the school year, with kids who couldn't pass the class 45 minutes at a time, in the summer heat, because of stiff competition? Many also tutor privately, but it's hard to get a lot of those gigs lined up at a time.

Teachers also do the following jobs in the summer and during the school year: babysitting, dog sitting, house sitting, teaching fitness classes, personal training, online teaching, selling baked goods, selling things on eBay, cashier at grocery stores, housekeeping at hotels, selling fruits and vegetables on the road, bartending, driving Uber/Lyft, selling clothes, candles, essential oils, nail wraps, dietary supplements etc. out of their homes, waitressing, working concessions at a baseball stadium, doing makeup, photography or DJing for weddings, legal assisting, dishwashing, playing in a band, selling real estate, driving a beverage cart at a golf course (where they say stupid shit like, "Oh you're a teacher! It must be nice to have the summer off!"), renting out a room in their house or apartment on Airbnb, working at the Renaissance Festival, managing property, delivering pizzas, cleaning porta potties for the forest service, painting faces at birthday parties, medical coding, lifting boxes for Amazon, cannabis coaching, choreographing, data entry, cleaning bathrooms in corporate offices, hairstyling, working as an EMT, professional mascot, selling fireworks, landscaping, working on an assembly line in a factory, zip line guide, parking attendant, vet tech, massage therapy, window washing, operating amusement park rides, calligraphy, and many simply moved back in with their parents to make ends meet.

20

"ESKETIT" AND OTHER HIP WORDS

"Smoke quarter pound to the face, esketit,
Everything that you done did, I done did it."

-Lil Pump, *one of the greatest
musical geniuses of our time*

Wanna be hip despite being over the age of 25? Throw a few of these vocabulary words into your next class discussion!

Bad- (adj) powerfully attractive or seductive

Example: They told him that on the morrow many princes and knights were going to the King's Court, there to joust and tourney for the love of his daughter, the Princess who was remarkably **bad**. *(Adapted from Pericles by Edith Nesbit)*

Baddie- (n) an irresistibly attractive woman

Example: The fair Ophelia! **Baddie**, *in thy orisons be all my sins remember'd. (Adapted from Hamlet by William Shakespeare)*

See also **bad bitch**

Big doink- (n) Cigar with tobacco removed and replaced with large quantities of marijuana

Example: "Yes dear, I'll be coming in," Leonce answered, with a glance following a misty puff of smoke. "Just as soon as I have finished this **big doink**." *(Adapted from The Awakening by Kate Chopin)*

See also **blunt**

Crank- (n) a female with an undiscriminating or unselective approach to choosing sexual mates

Example: Moll Flanders was born in Newgate, and during a life of continu'd variety for threescore years, besides her childhood, was twelve year a **crank**, *five times a wife, eight year a transported felon in Virginia, at last grew rich, liv'd honest, and died a penitent. (Adapted from Moll Flanders by Daniel Defoe, 1722)*

See also **fuck boy/boi**

Dank (adj/n)- very potent strains of marijuana; splendid

Example: Is this a pipe full of **dank** *which I see before me, the handle toward my hand? (Adapted from Macbeth by William Shakespeare)*

Deadass- (adj) in a sincere manner, serious

Example: My dear aunt, this is **deadass** *indeed. You need not be under any alarm. I will take care of myself, and of Mr. Wickham too. (Adapted from Pride and Prejudice by Jane Austen)*

Esketit- rap musician Lil Pump's made up version of the words "let's get it!" Used in place of those words or just shouted out at random intervals to alert passersby of your hipness

Example: This day we fight! By all that you hold dear on this good Earth, I bid you stand, Men of the West! **Esketit***! (Adapted from Lord of the Rings by J.R.R. Tolkien)*

Extra- (adj) behavior that is exceeding what is usual, proper, necessary, or normal

Example: "Maman, it's you who are being **extra** *now, not I," Lise's voice carolled through a tiny crack of the door at the side. (Adapted from The Brothers Karamazov by Fyodor Dostoyevsky)*

Fire- (n) very good of its kind, first-class, excellent

Example: The surgeon examined her pulse, and her wound, on which green leaves were laid and declared, "Who gave you this healing herb? It is **fire***!" (Adapted from Uarda by Georg Ebers)*

Flame- (v) to express a strongly held opinion about someone; to insult

Example: How are we to discover the ringleaders of those who **flamed** *me yesterday in the Circus, and of those among the youths in the stadium who have dared to express their vile disapproval by whistling in my very face? (Adapted from A Thorny Path by Georg Ebers)*

Fortnite- (n) a computer game that 15-year-old males are enamored with; the bane of a teacher's existence

Example: Before my body I throw on my warlike shield, lay on, and damn'd be him that first cries, "Do you play **fortnite***?" (Adapted from Macbeth by William Shakespeare)*

Fuck boy/boi- (n) a male with an undiscriminating or unselective approach to choosing sexual mates

Example: Pryer had done well to warn Ernest against promiscuous house to house visitation by way of being a **fuck boy***. (Adapted from The Way of All Flesh by Samuel Butler)*

See also **crank**

Gucci- (adj) favorable, enjoyable

Example: Blame where you must, be candid where you can; and be each critic of the **'Gucci Natur'd Man'***. (adapted from Epilogue to the Good Natur'd Man by Oliver Goldsmith)*

Kill- (v?) yelled out as a reaction to almost anything upsetting, disappointing or funny

Example: Mr. Darcy said, "She is tolerable, but not handsome enough to tempt me; I am in no humour at present to give consequence to young ladies who are slighted by other men," to which Mr. Bingley replied, **"Kill***." (Adapted from Pride and Prejudice by Jane Austen)*

Loud- (n) high quality, potent marijuana

*Example: Uncle Charles smoked such black twist that at last his nephew suggested to him to enjoy smoking his morning **loud** in a little outhouse at the end of the garden. (Adapted from A Portrait of the Artist as a Young Man by James Joyce)*

Sauce- (n) self-confidence, self-esteem

*Example: A Frenchman is self-assured because he regards himself personally, both in mind and body, as having a certain **sauce** which is irresistibly attractive to men and women. (Adapted from War and Peace by Leo Tolstoy)*

Shook- (n) the state of being mentally or emotionally disturbed by an outside circumstance

*Example: As Achilles wept for thinking of his dear comrade, he lay on his side, till at last he rose and went out as one most **shook**, to wander upon the seashore. (Adapted from The Iliad by Homer)*

Skrrt- (v?) Noise made by screeching automobile wheels; to move away from someone

*Example: The thing in the coffin writhed; and a hideous, blood-curdling **skrrt** came from the opened red lips. (Adapted from Dracula by Bram Stoker)*

Skunt-(n) a detestable human being; one who merits intense dislike

*Example: She may be fair, clever and well-heeled, but she is a **skunt**. (Adapted from Great Expectations by Charles Dickens)*

Slight work- (n) work that involves little difficulty or discomfort

*Example: The languages of Polynesia are **slight work** to smatter, though hard to speak with elegance. (Adapted from In the South Seas by Robert Louis Stevenson)*

Snatched- (adj) having a perfect or fashionable appearance

*Example: The **snatched** appearance of the lady included large-eyed prettiness which had the fixity of something impaled and shown under glass. (Adapted from The House of Mirth by Edith Wharton)*

Stunting- (v) to engage in attention-seeking behavior

Example: Occurring about once a month, it was a ritual believed to be mere **stunting***, in which war prisoners were hanged as a public spectacle and was a popular entertainment among schoolchildren. (Adapted from 1984 by George Orwell)*

Sus- (adj) short for *suspicious,* doubtful, questionable

Example: Let each of us wait at a gate of the palace with three Musketeers behind him; if we see a close carriage, at all **sus** *in appearance, let us fall upon it. (Adapted from* The Three Musketeers *by Alexandre Dumas)*

Thicc- (adj) having the curves of a well-proportioned feminine figure particularly in the hips and buttocks

Example: She had been supposed to have rather a good figure, but now she was out of fashion: a little too **thicc***, not enough like an adolescent boy. (Adapted from* Lady Chatterley's Lover *by D.H. Lawrence)*

Tough- (adj) excellent, first-rate

Example: Alas, poor Yorick! I knew him, Horatio. A fellow of infinite jest. His jokes were **tough***. (Adapted from Hamlet by William Shakespeare)*

Triggered- (adj) An emotional/psychological reaction caused by something that relates to an upsetting time in someone's life. This reaction often occurs in war veterans, people suffering from PTSD, depression, and other mental disorders but is irritatingly misused and overused by young people to express discomfort of any kind

Example: Though Birnam wood be come to Dunsinane, and thou opposed, being of no woman born, I am thus **triggered***. (Adapted from Macbeth by William Shakespeare)*

Woke- (adj) having or showing realization, perception, or knowledge about current affairs and politics

Example: Bodhisattvas were thought of as **woke** *and were generally regarded as persons who in their past lives cultivated virtues, underwent austerities, and various sorts of penance, and at length attained a complete* **wokeness** *by virtue of which they secured peace and eternal bliss. (Adapted from* The Religion of the Samurai *by Kaiten Nukariya)*

21

THIS IS WHY I'M SO "SALTY"

Did I Miss Anything?

Nothing. When we realized you weren't here
we sat with our hands folded on our desks
in silence, for the full two hours.
Everything. A few minutes after we
began last time a shaft of light suddenly descended and an
angel
or other heavenly being
appeared and revealed to us what
each woman or man must do
to attain divine wisdom in this life
and the hereafter
This is the last time the class will meet
before we disperse to bring the good news to all people on
earth.

-Tom Wayman

Students ask the same questions all day long, every day, and are shocked when they get an attitude from their teacher. "*Damn*, why are you so salty, Miss? I was just asking a question." Yes, and that question is one of the most irritating questions I am forced to hear all day long.

The worst questions they always ask:

"Is this for a grade?"

If I tell you that it's not going to be graded then you won't do it, right? So yeah, it's for a grade.

"Did I miss anything while I was out?"

Of course not! We stopped everything and stared at the wall, anxiously awaiting your return.

Instructions are on the board, at the top of the worksheet and have been explained multiple times. Student looks up from phone/takes out earbuds and asks, "What are we doing?"

You better ask somebody else because I might get violent if I have to explain this again.

"Are we gonna do anything fun today?"

Fun? I don't even know what that is. I purposefully make everything boring just to torture you!

"Why did you give me such a bad grade/fail me?"

This has nothing to do with earning points and effort. I grade based on how I feel about you personally, and I don't like you.

"Do I have to put my name on it?"

Of course not! I have memorized the handwriting of all 150 of my students just to save you the trouble of writing your name!

"Can we watch a movie today?"

Look, I would love nothing more than to get paid to show you movies every day. We watch them as much as we possibly can in an English class. But we have to do work sometimes, or I'll lose my job.

"What are we doing today?"

Thanks for asking. Even though it is written on the board, I love explaining it to each student individually!

"Can I go see another teacher?"

I want to say that you will miss part of my class but I know that you will tell me that their class is more important, so just go.

"Can you give me all my missing work?"

Even though all of the work is posted online every day, and all handouts are in the same location they have always been… sure! Let me save you the trouble and assemble all of that for you! I know you've been busy cutting class, so I really don't mind.

"Are we doing anything today?"

Of course not! We are going to do absolutely nothing, and it's going to be amazing.

"Why do we have to do this?"

Even though the powers that be make me post the objective of the lesson every day, and it is right in front of your face, I really, truly do not know why we are doing this.

"How many questions will there be on the test?"

Whatever number I say, you will complain about. You will say it is too few or too many questions. So I'm going to say I don't remember.

"How much is this worth?"

You're trying to determine if you really have to do it or not, right?

"Will there be an essay?"

You're only asking so that you can complain about it, so you'll just have to wait and see.

"Can we have a free day?"

I would love to give you a day to do nothing, and I can completely ignore you, but it is not really feasible. However, the closest I can come to this is to give you group work.

Student hands in paper and asks at the end of the same class, "Did you grade my paper?"

Seeing as how I have 150+ papers to grade, and I'm not a machine, no I did not grade your paper yet.

"Do I have to do this?"

What are you really asking me? Is this worth points? Is this worth a lot of points? Is this busy work? If you choose not to do this will you still pass? There is no way in hell I am answering those questions.

"Do I have to answer all of the questions?"
No, most of them are there just to make it look like we do stuff.

"What's my grade?"

Hold on, let me pull up that grade book I keep in my brain that updates minute by minute...

"Wait. What'd you just say? I wasn't listening."

I know they say honesty is a virtue, but in this case, you really should have gone with a lie.

"Do you have an iPhone charger?"

If I did have one, and I was willing to lend it out, I cannot even fathom the chaos that would ensue. Although if I lent it on a first come, first serve basis perhaps it would be an incentive to get here on time? (A girl can dream can't she?)

"Can we have class outside?"

Even if this were possible, and I wouldn't be viewed as a hippie by admin., it is hard enough holding your attention in a classroom made of cinderblocks. If we add sunshine, the chirping of birds, and a gentle breeze to the mix, I fear you will be lost forever.

"Is this test open-book?"

Has any test ever been open-book? If so, it either wasn't actually a test, or the teacher completely gave up on you.

"Do you have anything to eat/candy?"

I would never randomly hand out candy or snacks because I would become the person to go to for free candy/snacks. (Seriously, there was one teacher who became known for his surplus of Costco snacks, and students would gather from all over to request snacks from him. They began to expect the same from the rest of us. He was a shitty teacher, but the students all said he was their favorite because not only did he feed them, he did ridiculous things like make waffles in the middle of MATH class. We all hated him, and eventually, he was transferred. Also, a student recently asked me for a snack. I took out four different types of granola bars, and she replied, "Eww. I don't like any of those." I won't be offering anything anymore except knowledge and sarcasm.)

"Can we do this with a partner/in a group?"

You mean, can you do this with a student who will do all the work and let you put your name on it out of intimidation? Not today, Satan.

"Will this be on the test?"

Most of what I say and most of what we do in here is irrelevant. I just love the sound of my voice saying random shit.

Student walks in ten/fifteen/twenty minutes late and asks, "Did you mark me late?"

I see we are about to have the most insane argument there ever was.

22

JUST MENTION HARAMBE ONE MORE TIME

"Don't believe everything you read on the internet."

-Abraham Lincoln

A meme is a virally-transmitted symbol or idea. Most modern memes are photos with captions that are supposed to be funny. Memes are the bane of a teacher's existence. First of all, memes are a great way to get a student's attention. If you include a popular meme in your slideshow, the students will take note and praise you for your with-it-ness. But the popularity of memes changes quickly and if you want your slideshow to have the same effect, you will need to update your memes from year to year. Let me just say, ain't nobody got time fo dat![35] The worst part about memes is how obsessed the students become. They will write it on your whiteboards. They will scribble it on their homework. They will shout it out several times per class. The word "overkill" means nothing to them.

Take, for example, the "Cash Me Ousside /How Bow Dah" meme of 2016. This quote was spoken by 13-year-old Danielle Bregoli on an episode of The Dr. Phil Show. The show was about how Danielle's mother could not control her daughter's behavior which included stealing cars. Danielle's language was so indecipherable that her mom had to translate for the audience. When the audience is yelling at her for being a piece of shit, the girl replies, "Cash me ousside, how bow dah?" No one knew what the fuck she said so her mom jumped in with, "Catch her outside means she'll go outside and do what she has to do." The best part of this story is that when she did see audience members outside the studio, one of them punched her right in the face. The worst part of this story is that soon after the show aired a clip of the girl's "catch-phrase" went viral, and she got a record deal and a reality show. I'm not hip enough to know if this girl is considered a hero or a joke to young people, but I know they were fixated on this phrase and slipped it into conversation whenever they could.

You might recall back in early 2015; there was an insanely stupid debate on social media over a dress. It all started when a woman in Scotland sent her daughter a picture of a dress she was considering wearing to a wedding. They began arguing about what color the dress was which led to one of the wedding guests posting the picture on social media to ask for the opinion of others. According to her, "The dress was obviously blue and black." After all, she had seen it in person. The post received around 840,000 views in the first day and then increased tenfold.[36] Someone posted the dress to Twitter which caused the site to crash continuously. The argument, which became known as "Dressgate," exploded across the globe. Celebrities, politicians and government agencies shared their opinions. Eventually, the dress was the subject of 4.4 million tweets within 24 hours, and a Buzzfeed article about it had 37 million views.[37] I'm sure that you took part in this debate somehow. But ultimately, the ones who suffered the most, in my humble opinion, were teachers and other school staff. Whenever you felt you had had enough of #Dressgate, you simply took a break from social media. Maybe when a coworker or family member brought it up, you told them you didn't want to talk about it. That's not an option with kids. They were obsessed with this dress to an unnatural degree. It didn't matter what measures we took to get them to think about something else. The dress was all that mattered.

At first, I participated. I told them it looked white and gold to me, but with bad lighting. The white and gold people would cheer, and the blue and black people would explode. After a few days, when a kid would ask me what color I thought the dress was, I would only respond with, *"I don't care."* While the question of the dress does bring up fascinating topics such as perception and how the brain perceives color, that's not what I heard about, *ever*. I only heard 4 colors being shouted across the classroom, sometimes ending in physical fights. By the way, if you're interested, the dress was confirmed as royal blue and black by the manufacturer.[38]

Probably the worst meme to come out of 2016-2017 was Harambe. Harambe was a gorilla who was shot and killed at the Cincinnati Zoo after a child fell into his paddock. The story went viral because people blamed the kid's parents for not paying enough attention to him. A petition entitled "Justice for Harambe" was created on Change.org which called for authorities to hold the child's parents responsible for Harambe's death. Within 48 hours, the petition gained over 338,000 signatures.[39] A comedian tweeted, "Dicks out for Harambe!" afterward and chaos ensued. It became the most popular hashtag on Twitter and other social media outlets. On November 8th, 2016, many people posted photographs of paper election ballots with "Harambe" as a write-in candidate in the United States presidential election.[40] On February 6th, 2017, a Cheeto that supposedly resembled Harambe sold on eBay for $99,900.[41] In the winter of 2017, the Harambe madness showed no sign of slowing down in classrooms across the country. If a student didn't know an answer to a test question, they were sure to write "Harambe." If a marker was left anywhere near an unattended whiteboard, you would fully expect "Dicks out for Harambe" to appear. Kids feigned genuine concern for Harambe. When asked to write a 6-word memoir, several students included the words "Justice for Harambe." The meme became so irritating that one teacher began issuing lunch detention for any mention of Harambe. Thankfully the Harambe obsession has died down a bit, but I am always afraid of what is coming next. It will almost certainly be dumber and more aggravating.

Since I wrote this chapter a few months ago, there have already been more stupid memes such as the yanny/laurel debate (which I refuse to rehash), and "big doinks." This is just a YouTube video of an overweight teen smoking large blunts and calling them "big doinks." I hear the phrase shouted out all day long. The other meme that made me want to murder someone this year was the debate over this question, "Is water wet?" That debate had my students enraptured for weeks and made it exceedingly difficult to get anything done. It is hard enough holding the attention of young people in today's classroom. So the next time you think about posting a question which might cause a worldwide riot, please, *think of the children.*

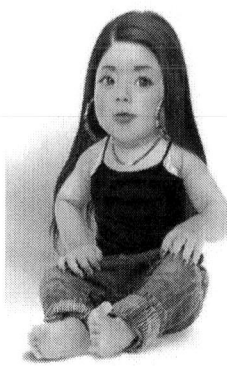

"Cash Me Outside"
costume for baby

★★★★☆ · 23 customer reviews

Price: $39.88 ✓Prime

Fit: Runs Large (33%) ▾

Size: 12-18 Months See Chart

Color: As Shown

In Stock.

Qty: 1 ▾

Add to Cart

or 1-Click Checkout

Buy now with 1-Click®

$39.88 + Free Shipping

EVERYONE IS AN HONORS STUDENT!

"No matter what the game or sport or competition, everybody wins. No child these days ever gets to hear those important character building words, 'You lost, Bobby.'
A lot of these kids never get to hear the truth about themselves until they're in their 20's when their boss calls them into their office and says, 'Bobby, clean the shit outta your desk and get the fuck outta here, you're a loser.' Of course, Bobby's parents can't understand why he can't hold a job. In school, he was always on the honor roll. Well, what they don't understand is that in today's schools, everyone is on the honor roll because, in order to be on the honor roll, all you really need to do is to maintain a body temperature somewhere roughly in the 90's."

-George Carlin

You've probably heard about games at the elementary level where every kid gets a trophy or ribbon for participation. Maybe you're aware that some elementary schools give honors certificates to each and every student at graduation. Maybe you've seen a "no score sports game" where no score is kept, and no winner is declared, to protect the delicate feelings of the losers. We tend to look the other way when faced with these practices because they are intended to protect the self-esteem of young kids—and because no one wants to be the dick who takes a kid's trophy away. But this mentality is spreading to upper grades, and it is making my job suck even more.

In the U.S. we have outrageous grade inflation that has seen a 28% rise in A's since the sixties. In fact, almost half of all high school students have an A average, even though the average SAT score continues to fall.[42] Many of these kids are really performing at a C average, but have pushy parents or have learned how to work the system to get that A.

No one ever asks teachers what they think of an idea before they thrust it onto them. The reason must be because they *know* their ideas are shitty and they don't want to deal with the pushback. They want to be able to say they are breaking ground with their forward thinking educational models (that are usually trashed within a few years) and they want that data! We are their guinea pigs, forced to try every idea that pops into their heads.

The latest educational experiment determined to "level the playing field" and encourage high self-esteem for all is the all honors model. When they first rolled this one out in my school, all 9th and 10th graders had one option for English class: Honors. The kids who read at a 2nd grade level and the kids who got perfect scores on the PSAT had one option: to study the same curriculum, use the same materials and learn at the same pace (actually they would tell you that all of these would be different according to ability level and that I would need to plan all that in advance). So why are they even in the same class in the first place? In 11th and 12th grade the choices were Honors or Advanced Placement (AP) English. Higher achieving kids took AP and lazy kids, or kids with lower ability levels, stayed in "Honors." One of the first problems that arose in 9th and 10th grade was that higher achieving students complained of boredom to their parents (and rightfully so). Enough parents complained and "Pre-AP" classes were created for the 9th and 10th grade, but spaces were limited, and you had to sign up in advance of the school year. These basically became the new Honors classes while the Honors classes were where the kids with "regular" abilities went. Kids who didn't get the memo about the "Pre-AP" classes ended up in the same classes as a wide range of ability levels.

Before we get to why this is a horrible idea, let's examine why anyone would think this is a good idea. "Mixed-ability classes" are meant to encourage patience and understanding. Theorists hope that the true honors level students will inspire and motivate the lower level students and that honors kids will learn "tolerance and the understanding and acceptance of differences."[43]

"Academically, higher-level students can help push lower-level students by modeling and encouraging them. This builds higher-level students' skills in consolidating information and mentoring others. It also exposes lower-level students to some of the higher-level thinking questions and problem-solving skills they might not observe if they remained in a low-level group."[44]

"All honors classes" are mainly meant to build the self-esteem of kids who do not usually get to have the honors label, and this is what my school focuses on the most.

This model is not a new concept; however, there is a reason it never really caught on until now. Research shows that grouping has almost no effect on academic performance among students of varying achievement levels. In my experience, this model holds *everyone* back. Honors students are bored, and lower level students are intimidated or fall behind. Administration's solution to this is to provide more work for the Honors kids and allow less work to be completed by lower level kids. When I tried that, the Honors kids complained that it wasn't fair (and it wasn't) and the lower level kids were embarrassed. Now everyone knew who was really an "honors student" which defeated the whole damn purpose. When I reported this situation, I was told to provide extra work for the Honors students who finished early, but tell them that they were merely getting a head start on a future assignment. Then I was either to excuse the lower level kids from that future assignment or just never grade it at all.

WHUT? Basically, I was giving the honors kids busy work and lying to them about its importance.

As far as the material we study, the books are either too easy or way too hard. I was told to assign specific books to specific students. So Geraldine got a version of Homer's *Odyssey* which was at a college level of difficulty. Bob got the graphic novel which had one sentence per page. For most of the assignments, they couldn't work together, so they ended up being separated anyway. *And that is what most of them wanted.* They wanted to be separated because the higher level kids were angry that they had so much more reading to do than the other kids, and the lower level kids were embarrassed that they were reading a picture book. I was advised to give them a choice of either book at this point. Some would *want* the challenge of the literal translation of Homer's *Odyssey*.

Now the whole class was doing the graphic novel.

Geraldine's book:

Book I

ARGUMENT: *Minerva's Descent to Ithaca*

> The poem opens within forty-eight days of the arrival of Ulysses in his dominions. He had now remained seven years in the island of Calypso, when the gods assembled in council proposed the method of his departure from thence, and his return to his native country. For this purpose it is concluded to send Mercury to Calypso, and Pallas immediately descends to Ithaca. She holds a conference with Telemachus, in the shape of Mentes, king of the Taphians; in which she advises him to take a journey in quest of his father Ulysses, to Pylos and Sparta, where Nestor and Menelaüs yet reigned; then, after having visibly displayed her divinity, disappears. The suitors of Penelope make great entertainments, and riot in her palace till night. Phemius sings to them the return of the Grecians, till Penelope puts a stop to the song. Some words arise between the suitors and Telemachus, who summons the council to meet the day following.

THE man for wisdom's various arts renown'd,
Long exercised in woes, O Muse! resound;
Who, when his arms had wrought the destined fall
Of sacred Troy, and razed her heaven-built wall,
Wandering from clime to clime, observant stray'd,
Their manners noted, and their states survey'd.
On stormy seas unnumber'd toils he bore,
Safe with his friends to gain his natal shore:
Vain toils! their impious folly dared to prey
On herds devoted to the god of day;
The god vindictive doom'd them never more
(Ah, men unbless'd!) to touch that natal shore.
Oh, snatch some portion of these acts from fate,
Celestial Muse! and to our world relate.
Now at their native realms the Greeks arrived;
All who the wars of ten long years survived,
And 'scaped the perils of the gulfy main.
Ulysses, sole of all the victor train,
An exile from his dear paternal coast,
Deplored his absent queen and empire lost.

r 45

Bob's book:

Oh yeah, I forgot to mention that 25% of these classes are composed of Special Ed. kids. So I have to plan, within one class period, for honors kids, on-level kids, below level kids, and Special Ed. kids. And be available to help them all at any time during class. This makes a lot of sense.

To summarize, I have students with very different ability levels and varying degrees of work ethic in the same class. They are all called honors students. They have different books, and assignments and tend to separate themselves based on their comfort level. Some students get graded more harshly than others based on their capabilities. They can't really work together because they are not working on the same assignments and the lower level kids do not want to ask the others for help because they are embarrassed. When someone brought up the fact that all the kids shouldn't get honors credit for the class because some are doing a lot less work and are being graded easier, it was proposed that the lower level kids would get less credit for the course. So if the kids are pretty much in separate classes (separate materials, abilities, and credit) within the same room... *perhaps they should just be in different classes to begin with?*

24

YOU CAN'T REASON WITH CRAZY

"Don't fuck with teachers.
They make no money.
They get up at 6:00 AM to drive
their 15-year-old cars to a
cruddy building knee-deep in teenage hormones.
You cannot scare them.
The part of them that is capable
of fear was burned away years ago
by terrible teachers' lounge coffee.
All they want is healthcare, a livable wage,
and just once, a class that doesn't laugh the first time they hear
'Uranus.' "

-Seth Meyers

I asked my teacher followers to provide their best words of advice for new teachers. I personally find this list to be helpful for new parents too! Here is a good overview of responses:

"Have a plan for self-care practices in place before even starting the school year."

"Don't do it. Just don't do it."

"You must have forgiveness, or you may just lose your mind."

"Believe in the power of mental health days."

"Carry aspirin on you at all times."

"Document everything."

"Don't take anything home unless you'll lose your job if you don't do it!"

"Be afraid, be very afraid!"

"Teach overseas where kids want to learn."

"Don't overthink it, you are probably doing more good than harm."

"Remember that you are part educator and part entertainer."

"Never work later than an hour past dismissal."

"Don't drown yourself for the sake of keeping up just because someone down the hall looks like they have it all together. They don't, they've just got more experience hiding it."

"Don't take anything too seriously. Education, administrators, and technology change too often to take anything on the job too seriously."

"Be picky with your school and district, and get yourself out the second you realize it's not a good fit."

"Don't do it."

"Even if you have a bad year- don't leave the profession. There's a new year coming to start again. Don't underestimate the power of a fresh start!"

"Don't be their friend, but do be supportive."

"Make teacher friends. No one else gets it... or even believes you sometimes."

"Get out NOW."

"Teach Phys Ed."

"Pick your battles."

"Lots of wine."

"You are more than your evaluation!"

"Don't compare yourself to Pinterest."

"Start training your bladder to hold it till the end of the day!"

"Don't do it."

"*Don't.*"

"Take care of yourself and your family first."

"Keep a teaching memory box. Fill it with all of the good things that happen."

"Don't follow other teachers' bad habits."

"Run."

"Buy a new liver."

"Therapy and meds."

"Have a back-up plan."

"Don't ever forget why you chose to teach in the first place!"

"Run far, far away... as fast as you can."

"Your first few years keep your mouth shut and your eyes open."

"Don't teach. Just don't."

"Get a good psychiatrist."

"Be careful what you write in notes to parents, it can come back to haunt you."

"Don't take it personally."

"It. Is. Just. A. Job. It is NOT your whole life nor does it define you."

"Be ready for anything. Look at the assignment below. What grade would you give this? According to my district's official writing rubric it deserves at least a C for effort."

"Your kids won't remember your lessons (sorry to tell you that) no matter how many hours you put into them. However, they will always remember how you made them feel!"

"Literally pick any other job. Seriously."

"Try not to become an alcoholic."

"You don't have to grade everything they turn it. Count it as 'participation points.'"

"Be real. Be honest."

"Say hello to each student by name as they walk in. That acknowledgment of presence is key."

"Don't be afraid to ditch the lesson and let student interest take over. It might be the best and most insightful lesson ever."

"Don't tie a wet shoelace when it's not raining outside."

"Soon you will reach a point where nothing -- absolutely nothing – will surprise you. When that happens, welcome, my friend."

"Every time you say no to someone else, you say yes to yourself."

"Stay out of the faculty room."

"Don't come in thinking you know everything. That's the quickest way to get on every teacher's nerves."

"Prepare yourself to be a special education teacher even if you're not trained for it. No one warned me."

"Learn to accept that absolutely nothing makes sense in public education. Nothing. An easy problem will have the most complicated solution, and it will drive you mad if you dwell on it."

"The relationships you build with your students will most likely be the reason you continue to stay. It is for me, and despite all the hardships, it's enough."

"Find a rich husband/wife."

"Change your major."

"Buy bigger pants because you will gain at least a pant size between food at work and alcohol."

"What you do now will have an impact on some now, but on others later. Don't feel you haven't made a difference even if you don't see it. You make the difference each day."

"Go with the chaos! If you try to control chaos, it erupts in your face."

"Prepare to be broke."

"God bless you."

"Start each day fresh. Even if one of your students was horrible the day before, greet that student with positivity and grace. Let them know that you will not hold bad behavior against them."

"Keep the tissues and garbage can far away from your desk."

"Start growing tougher skin now. You'll need it."

"Laugh with colleagues and laugh with kids."

"Runnnnnnnnnnnnnn!"

"Don't be hard on yourself. You're going to make mistakes."

"Run 🏃🏃🏃🏃👉"

"Join a wine club."

"Be a part of the solution. Revolutions are built on the backs of revolutionaries."

"Fake it til you make it!"

"Come to the realization that you can't save them all. I know you want to try to and that's awesome, but it isn't reality. I've cried more than a few times this year because I can't save all my kids like I would like to. *You are only one person.*"

"Never do phone calls. Emails are best because it's documented."

"Don't take what the kids say personally but don't be afraid to show them you are human and have emotions. The ones you think hate you are usually the ones who love and need you the most."

"Be flexible, like an Olympic gymnast and Gumby had a baby."

"Survive."

"Always try new things. New lessons, new games, new grade levels, new schools. Don't get stuck doing the same stuff over and over again."

"Put your desk out of view of the door because sometimes you just need to sit for a second and don't need to be in the eye line of an administrator walking past your door."

"Nap during your planning period."

"Trust your instincts. Teachers who really care make decisions that they feel are best for their students. Anything can be a teachable moment."

"Don't count on grants or teacher loan forgiveness."

"There is no ideal demographic of kids to teach! The best school environment is one with competent teachers and competent administration that has your back."

"Don't try to reinvent the wheel! There are so many great resources out there that you can tweak to fit the needs of your students without spending hours and hours planning an original lesson from scratch."

"Drink water frequently. Eat breakfast. Actually eat lunch your lunch break."

"Life calls you to a certain place, time, and a feeling. Please honor that because there are people there counting on you to take the reins of this wild horse. I'm not sure if you'll get paid what you deserve, but the lives you change will pay you back times 10."

"You'll be miserable if you don't have a sense of humor and learn to laugh at yourself every once in a while."

"Get out while you still can!"

"You'll get better at it faster than you think. Every year is different. Actually, every week is different. One week you might be googling 'how to transition out of teaching,' and the next week you might have such a zest for some idea and be reinvigorated."

"Everyone has something to offer you- the old folks, the middle of the road folks, and the newbies! Listen to them!"

"Whatever expectations you have, throw them out the window. Your first year will not go as planned. Roll with it. Learn to be flexible. Forgive quickly. Don't let your anger and frustration from today bleed into tomorrow."

"Pre-frontal lobotomy required."

"Make friends with the office manager/everyone who works in the front office. Buy them coffee. They will save your ass on the regular."

"Pick another career while you can."

"Don't do it."

"RUN."

"Pick the state you work in very, very carefully."

"Smile and nod, and then do whatever you know is right in your classroom."

"Don't trust anyone who speaks at length during staff meetings."

"Make a budget and start a Roth right away ($50 a month at 22 will grow to a sizable amount by 30)."

"Find a good bar."

"If you're doing it because you love science or literature or math, don't do it. It will never be Dead Poet's Society. You have to teach because you like the kids or it'll never work."

"It's okay to cry."

"Make sure all the liquor store employees know you by name."

"Run."

"Your master teacher is going to hate you. Don't let them make you feel inferior!"

"Know your rules, enforce them- period."

"Don't be afraid to look like an idiot, because you'll have fun and they might learn."

"Always watch your back. Document everything. *Everything.*"

"Know administrators will judge you for every little thing you do or don't do. They will always find *something* you are doing wrong."

"Arguing with a teenager is like wrestling a hog: both of you will get dirty, but the hog is gonna enjoy it."

"Run Forrest RUN 🏃!"

"Know how you will react when a kid says, 'fuck you!' (Even an elementary schooler)"

"Expect to say something stupid in front of students."

"Kids and their parents can be really mean! Just remember, you aren't their problem, they have their own problems and are taking it out on you!"

"Add tea tree oil to your shampoo and lice will avoid your head altogether."

"Have your person in your building you can vent to with no judgment. They will remind you you're not insane."

"Don't do it. Run! Go be a cashier!"

"Be kind, be honest, be silly but also be straightforward and take shit from no one."

"You'll encounter stupid shit every day. Learn to laugh."

"Get out now!"

"Allocate time every evening where you allow yourself to *stop giving a fuck*. In other words, switch off, do not allow yourself to obsess over students, lesson plans or whatever bullshit happened that day. Easier said than done but that mental space is valuable."

"Don't be afraid. Bad things will happen, but kids are stronger than you think."

"You can't reason with crazy. Show as much grace to the crazy as possible and move on."

"There are days when you think you can't do this job for one more minute but then you get the faintest hint that you do matter and that these kids need you and one day they may actually value something you taught them. Hold on tightly to that feeling."

"Run fast and far!"

"Put your own family first."

"Only teach if you can't imagine being happy doing anything else."

"Quit NOW! Get your exit plan NOW! This job sucks and is only getting worse!"

"Stop being so fucking awkward because these kids will shred you apart one organ at a time."

"Know that sometimes you will be sad. Instead of anger, frustration, or apathy, there will be sadness that it has to be the way it is. It is sad that so many kids have shitty home lives. It is sad that so many parents don't care. It is sad that kids are so angry and take it out on teachers, the people who actually care. It is sad that so many kids refuse to put down their phones and try to connect with someone in real time. It's sad that the good kids get overshadowed by the difficult ones. It is sad that teachers who are truly passionate and talented are being driven out of schools in huge numbers for the sake of their own health. It is sad that this job is as hard as it is... *because it shouldn't be.*"

"If you don't go home at least once a semester and sob uncontrollably for half an hour, you're doing it wrong."

"Remember that some students understand the work and effort you put in every day of your lives and are extremely thankful to have you all around!"

"After all the blood, sweat and tears you will give, some students just won't care. It may feel like a slap in the face, but it is important to remember that it has nothing to do with you and there is only so much you can do."

"It's easier to give up than to fight the apathy. Tomorrow will be better and so will you."

"It's so emotionally draining to be on the defensive all day long. Each day it seems like our aspirations grow farther and farther away. The joy and hope I felt with becoming a teacher shrinks and shrinks. Then there are random glimpses of hope like a kid's face lighting up when they figure something out, or a parent that sends in a thank you note just because, or overhearing one kid say they love your class and knowing that we can affect at least one life. Be prepared for the difficult but keep those hopes and dreams alive."

"With all of the inconsistencies that many students face at home, school should be a constant for them. Set rules, set policies, etc. There are no consistent upholding of policies (disciplinary, academic, scheduling, whatever) and it is extremely frustrating."

"It's true soul work, serving our students in the classroom. But remember you are human too."

"Some honestly won't give a shit. Some will complain, no matter how hard you work, not knowing how hard it is. We are not appreciated, especially by parents (who should know). You must see it as a mission. No mission was ever easy. It's not just a job. And one kid who gets it is enough. *If we don't do it, who will?*"

"You will see your friends' homes and salaries become a lot better than yours. You will see them vacationing, or getting free paid vacations from work, or working from home. Constantly teachers are portrayed horribly in the media. Stay strong."

"The cellphone will be the bane of your existence. If you can find a way to control that you will have a much easier time."

"Be prepared to work with a curriculum that in no way shapes or fosters free thinkers but rather mindless robots programmed for the purpose of performing well on a test. This is probably not what you signed up for nor is there any joy in it. Build in small lessons and moments of what you truly want to teach as much as you can."

"Many students have home lives that are rough. Remember that you may be all they have. You could be saving lives. *It is that serious."*

"We shouldn't have to deal with what we face, and that message needs to be sent. This is a profession that has run people into the ground. Speak out about it whenever you can."

"Be prepared for every possible scenario. I literally had a kid wrestle me over a folder and then proceed to bang his head and arms against a concrete wall. How would you handle that situation? Whatever you come up with, you're wrong."

"Exercise your right to protest! Especially for all of us who can't."

"Don't marry a teacher. It's too much exhaustion and complaining for one house."

"Teach in a prison. It's much nicer."

"If you are thinking about quitting, try another school. If it is not for you, then by all means quit. However, don't judge teaching just based on one school or one type of school."

"It's getting harder and harder and worse and worse. But the kids can be so great. And some of them grow. Become confident. You can literally see them blossom before your eyes. You see them and no one else does. It's special, our job. We're lucky. No matter how bad the pay, no matter how shitty we're treated...we're fucking lucky. No one knows how being a teacher feels, except you."

And here's my advice: Keep in mind that no year of your career will ever be as hard as your first year. You're not tough enough yet. In the beginning, you take everything personally. How could it *not* be personal? You're putting all of yourself into this job, and you get a ton of negative feedback. Remember that a few years from now you won't care about those things. Eventually, you will be confident in your abilities and it won't matter what administration thinks or what students write online. You also have to put in a huge amount of work during that first year. You are starting from scratch, developing all the materials, and making lessons your own. You will be spending all of your time developing lessons and grading, and you might think that you will always have to devote this much time to it. But you won't. You'll become more efficient.

And you are probably over-grading. New teachers tend to give a ton of feedback for every student on every assignment. It is admirable. But most students don't give a shit about your feedback, and that is the reality of it. I see teachers sitting there writing two or three paragraphs of feedback on each paper. With each new assignment that means 150 papers to grade. You will be spending your whole life grading. Meanwhile, most kids look at their grade and put the paper right into the recycling bin. I have students turn their papers in online, and I let them know that if they want my written feedback they need to bring me a printed copy. They must put in just a minuscule amount of effort to show me that they actually want the feedback and not just a grade. Out of 150 students, I usually get around 10 printed essays. I save a lot of time by not writing comments for kids that won't read them.

There's also a bit of a hazing period that every teacher goes through. When I went through it, I was very angry about it. New teachers need more support, and part of the hazing is that you're given the worst classes that no one else wants. That doesn't really make sense because you're new. You don't know what you're doing. Why wouldn't they give you the classes with better behaved kids? The reason is that the other teachers have put in their time, are burnt out, and practically refuse to put up with that kind of shit. They've paid their dues. It's your turn to prove yourself. You're also going to be talked into running a million clubs and should do some of that to show that you're "a team player." But once you have a couple of years of experience and you're considered permanent part of the department or the school, then it's somebody else's turn to be treated like a piece of shit. It ain't right, but it's the way it is.

Most importantly, expect the crazy. Be ready for the crazy. Be crazy in return. Get silly. Get stupid. Have fun even when there is no room for it. Don't take anything too seriously. Laugh at EVERYTHING. Be flexible. Don't be a hard-ass. Be honest with your students about everything and they will appreciate it and you. Tell them the standardized test they have to take is stupid and a waste of time and doesn't measure their worth. Then try to squeeze in a lesson about something you are truly passionate about, even if it's only for five minutes. And remember there is truth in the fact that you never really know who you are getting through to. So many teenagers have that permanently pissed off look. I always think they hate my class and me but then they will write me a letter or tell another teacher how much they love my class and I am blown away. You really can't judge kids too quickly. Some are much tougher to crack than others, but almost all of them are capable of being reached in some way. Again, be real with them. Tell them you don't understand why they seem mad all the time. Remind them that you aren't trying to torture them, you are just trying to do your job and make it as painless as possible. And hopefully, you'll both learn something from one another along the way.

And don't try to be a hardcore disciplinarian if it doesn't come naturally to you. I am a very passive person by nature, and when I try to be strict, it fails immediately. What works for me is having honest conversations about my feelings and my struggles. Students usually appreciate where I'm coming from and back off. They like being talked to like adults. Like real people. Remember how much it sucked when you were their age. Don't say shit like, "What are you complaining about? This is the best time of your life!" Maybe it was *for you,* but your experience is not everyone's experience. For some of them, due to their home life and various other factors, this is actually the worst time of their life. I tell them that. I tell them that it gets better when you can make your own choices and live your own life. I wouldn't go back for all the money in the world. Do you know how comforting that is for a lot of kids to hear? Just be yourself and be real and the kids will reciprocate. I mean, a lot of them will still be total dicks. But underneath they are grateful, and they don't even know it.

25

ANNUAL TORTURE NIGHT

"The teacher isn't here tonight?

You're the teacher?

What is this some kind of fucking joke or something?

You look about 12-years-old!"

-Parent on Back to School Night

Some call it Back to School Night, while others refer to it as Open School Night, Open House, or Meet the Teacher Night. I call it *cruel and unusual punishment* because that's what it feels like. After a nine-hour school day, teachers are expected to stick around another seven hours to prepare their classrooms and themselves for the random adults who might saunter in at their leisure (yes, there is a schedule, but that does not seem to mean much).

I understand the need for conferences for elementary school kids, and for older kids who are struggling. But this evening is not intended to be for individual families. It is for the teacher to put on a little show so the parents can look us up and down and decide if what their kid reports at home about us is accurate. And I don't think most parents want to be there either. After their own hectic work day, I'm sure the last thing they want to do is go to school.

The school day is nine periods long, so we go through a little mock school day to show the parents what their kid's schedule is like. I prepare a ten-minute long presentation for all five of my classes, and try not to talk too fast so there will be no dead air at the end. You never want to leave any room for discussion or questions because someone will inevitably stump you, yell at you, and blame you for things that aren't your fault, or try to talk about their own kid in front of everyone else. I try to be interesting and witty, yet serious and professional, but I end up feeling (and looking like, I'm sure), a circus monkey.

The problem is that parents of kids who *desperately* need parent involvement usually do not attend. The parents who do attend are both respectful and quiet, overly involved and of the helicopter variety, rude, or just plain nuts (or some combination of these). The helicopter type will write down every single thing I say, make confused faces, nod in agreement, and jot down questions and concerns. These queries will often be awkwardly interjected into my presentation.

"Yeah, excuse me, my daughter said _____ about the essay deadlines in this class. I want to follow up about that."

These parents almost always try to squeeze in a mini-conference in the three minutes I have between "classes." They'll corner me and get really close to my face and ask for feedback on their kid. (What makes this especially difficult is that I've only known their kid for a few weeks, and can't remember their names yet. So I have to pretend that I know who the eff they're talking about.) Some will just want to let me know how brilliant their kid is and will list their accomplishments. Some of them will want to show off their knowledge: "Oh I remember that book from college. I wrote a fancy analysis of blah blah blah..." Others will tell the whole group that the work seems too easy for their kid, or that their kid already read all the books in the curriculum during the summer.

But the rude ones are so unbelievably rude you can't believe it. "I would like to know where you got your degree from."

"How many years have you been teaching?"

"What makes you qualified to teach students of this ability level?"

This is when the sweat really starts to pour down my back. I try to adequately answer these bullshit questions and quickly move on with my little song and dance. But then someone will yell out, "When are you going to discuss the assignments? I already know/don't care about this other stuff!" or, "This class seems boring. How will you hold their interest?"

Can someone explain to me why I have to answer this politely? It's just more shit eating. I do it all day long when kids say whatever the fuck they feel to me and I have to be polite and respectful in return. Then their parents come by and do the adult version of the same thing, and I have to continue to smile and "be the adult." This is why some teachers *snap*!

Then there are the parents who spend the entire time on their phones.

In fact, I had a "class" where only one parent showed up. She sat in the front row and did not lift her head from her phone the entire ten minutes. It was the most awkward situation ever. I was basically talking to someone who was barely there. At one point I paused, because it was just so absurd, and without looking up she responded, "I'm listening." Another time there were two moms who sat in the front row and had a very friendly and rambunctious chat during my presentation. If these were students, I would have told them to knock it off or get out. But am I supposed to do the same with parents? Many teachers would say yes, tell them to shut their stupid mouths or leave while most administrators would advise me to suck it up as we do with everything else.

The last type of fascinating parent that shows up on BTSN are the super lonely/truly nutty ones. On a normal day, in a totally different, not work-related situation, these people would be a real hoot. But in the classroom, you have to listen to them, pretend to understand them, and it is way harder to escape the weirdness. There isn't really anywhere to go. And you feel for their children.

The really wacky ones come in a number of shapes and sizes. There are the close talkers. They stand a half an inch from your face and follow you as you back up into the wall. They usually have shockingly bad breath. Then there is your new best friend. They have all of the same interests as you and would love to get coffee, say, tomorrow night? There is the single dad (or even worse, the not so single dad), who asks you for a date under the guise of discussing their kid, otherwise known as a *slimeball*. There are the amateur writers who would love it if you would edit their shitty novel. There is the parent who has a restraining order against them and isn't legally allowed near their child or the school, who takes the opportunity to glean information about their kid.

That actually happened to me. A woman filibustered the entire presentation and then after everyone left she proceeded to ask me very personal questions about her son. She followed me out to the parking lot, and I pretty much had to cut her off by jumping into my car and slamming the door (and locking it of course). The next day when I mentioned how enthusiastic his mother was, the woman's son turned pale as a ghost. He explained that she is mentally ill and not allowed within a certain distance of him. Sounded about right.

The best part of BTSN is the drive home with the windows down, airing my sweaty self out like a wet dog. There is a triumph in knowing that I don't have to do that shit for a whole year. *But why do I have to do that circus monkey show at all?*

26

THERE'S NO JUSTICE IN RESTORATIVE JUSTICE

"Teachers are afraid of the principal. The principal is afraid of the superintendent. The superintendent is afraid of the school board. The school board is afraid of the parents. The kids aren't afraid of anybody."

-Robert L. Bailey

Just like the idea of all honors classes and world peace, the idea of "restorative justice" is a beautiful concept. However, the consequences of this newest form of edushit has been a total shit-show for teachers and well-behaved students.

Rather than punish a student through suspension, restorative justice asks the misbehaving student to reflect on his or her behavior, take responsibility, and resolve to do better in the future. This process often involves students and teachers sitting in a "restorative circle," in which the guilty student listens to the views of their peers and then gets to speak his or her mind. Other restorative practices include writing a letter of apology or verbally apologizing, participating in a fundraiser, or writing a speech or reflection paper. Although many students do see writing anything as a form of punishment, most of these consequences are not really severe enough considering the offenses the students are guilty of. Plus, there are not enough resources to properly oversee these programs and students usually just don't do them.

The Restorative Justice movement in schools became popular a few years ago as a backlash against zero-tolerance discipline policies in schools. Zero-tolerance policies have led to larger numbers of youths being out of school due to suspension. It seems counterintuitive to force a student to miss school in response to troublesome behavior. There is also a racial/ethnic disparity in which students receive punishments and the severity of the punishment. Suspension is also strongly linked to failure to graduate and a higher likelihood of ending up in jail.[47]

Thanks to talking circles and peer juries, "young people are now taking control of the environment," former Education Secretary Arne Duncan announced in a 2014 speech at Howard University. "It's sort of a counterintuitive thing for many of us as adults, but the more we give up power, the more we empower others, often the better things are," Duncan added. "And empowering teenagers to be part of the solution, having them control the [classroom] environment, control the culture, be the leaders, listening to them, respecting them — when we do that, wonderful things happen for kids in communities that didn't happen historically."[48] This sounds great *in theory*, but of course, as with everything suggested to us in education, in practice it is a whole different ball game.

The days of removing a disruptive kid from class are over. "Problems in class can take days, even weeks to resolve as schools coordinate talking circles around the schedules of teachers, principals, counselors, parents, and even campus police — all of whom must take time out and meet to deal ever-so-delicately with a single problem student."[49]

One Denver teacher told Chalkbeat magazine that under the new discipline policy, students had threatened to harm or kill teachers, 'with no meaningful consequences.'[50] After Oklahoma City Public Schools adopted restorative practices, one teacher told the Oklahoman that, "We were told that referrals would not require suspension unless there was blood."[51]

The NYC School Survey of teachers and students found that restorative practices increased violence in 50% of schools, gang activity increased in 39% of schools and for drug and alcohol use there was a 37% increase while only 7% of schools improved.[52]

If you didn't see the results of surveys like this or hear the experiences of teachers firsthand, you might think these practices are working. Many urban school districts are reporting fewer suspensions since adopting the non-punitive approach. But that doesn't necessarily mean kids are behaving better- the schools just aren't reporting it! "An audit last year by New York's Office of the State Comptroller reviewed incidents of violence in 10 public schools in New York City and found that nearly one-third of all incidents went unreported. According to the review, school officials failed to include over 400 reportable incidents on forms that are used to tally incidents of violence, and many of the incidents that were reported were not correctly categorized."[53] Many children in New York City schools were hit, kicked, and bullied by fellow students while administrators stood by, according to a recent class-action lawsuit.

While the numbers look good, many districts across the country are seeing a dramatic increase in classroom disruptions and violence. In 2015, the Chicago Teachers Union complained that the city's revised discipline policy had left teachers struggling to control unruly kids. "It's just basically been a totally lawless few months," one teacher told the Chicago Tribune.[54]

In Syracuse N.Y. teachers say teens are fighting more, cursing out teachers and roaming the halls under the more lenient behavior policy. They even see increasingly violent behavior among elementary school children. While the approach might be nice in theory, Syracuse Teachers Association President Kevin Ahern said in a recent letter to the Syracuse Post-Standard, it has created a "systemic inability to administer and enforce consistent consequences for violent and highly disruptive student behaviors" that "put students and staff at risk and make quality instruction impossible."[55]

Ramsey County Attorney John Choi of St. Paul, Minnesota, described how the number of assaults against teachers doubled from 2014 to 2015 and called the situation a "public health crisis."[56] In front of the U.S. Commission on Civil Rights, a former Philadelphia teacher testified that a student said, "I'm going to torture you. I'm doing this because I can't be removed."

Los Angeles Unified School District sees a similar increase in campus offenses after its school superintendent sought to reduce suspensions. Even threats against teachers are ignored.[57] "I was terrified and bullied by a fourth-grade student," a teacher at a Los Angeles Unified School District school recently told the Los Angeles Times. "The student told me to 'Back off, bitch.' I told him to go to the office and he said, 'No, bitch and no one can make me.' "[58]

"My teachers are at their breaking point," wrote Art Lopez, the union representative for a middle school in L.A., to union official Colleen Schwab in a letter obtained by The Times. "Everyone working here is highly aware of how the lack of consequences has affected the schools. Teachers with a high number of students with discipline issues are walking a fine line between extreme stress and an emotional meltdown."[59]

In California's Santa Ana public school district, "middle schoolers now regularly smoke pot in bathrooms — some even in class — and attack staff — spitting on teachers, pelting them with eggs, even threatening to stab them," according to the Orange County Register.[60] A recent teacher's union survey reveals that 65% of Santa Ana educators said the softer discipline system is not working. Dozens of teachers have filed hostile-work-environment complaints just weeks after "empowering teenagers," San Diego Public Schools witnessed a surge in violent assaults. At Lincoln High School, for example, students reported frequent campus fighting. In just one recent month, there were several arrests, including one involving a butcher knife, according to local TV news reports. School officials confirm at least 16 cases of battery in just the first few months of the school year.[61]

"There have been serious threats against teachers," Oakland High School science teacher Nancy Caruso told the Christian Science Monitor, and yet the students weren't expelled. She notes a student who set another student's hair on fire who received a "restorative talk" in lieu of suspension.

Instead of being kicked out of school or suffering other serious punishments, even repeat offenders can negotiate the consequences for their bad behavior, which usually involves writing a paper and having "dialogue sessions." Yet in my experience, no one checks to see if the kid wrote the papers or attended any sessions. Not that they would have helped without other means of discipline as well.

The following is a list of behavioral incidents from schools across the country that received no consequences:

Students smoke pot in the hall, stairwell or even in class with no consequence.

Students have sex in the hallway, stairwell or bathroom with no consequence.

Several pregnant teachers have been assaulted *with no consequence.*

Boys will pull out their junk for no apparent reason, and with no consequence.

Student shoved the teacher, and instead of being punished for his actions the teacher was told, "Stay out of his way, you know how he is."

A child put a plastic bag over another kid's head and tried to suffocate him. He thought it was hilarious. The principal said, "I guess you learned your lesson, right son? Now go play."

A 3rd grader jumped up on a table and drank   hand sanitizer during a standardized test to get out of it. He received no consequence and didn't have to take the test.

A student hit/scratched his teacher, drawing blood, with no consequence.

A kid wrote how he wanted to kill his teacher multiple times on a piece of paper in class with no consequence.

Teacher caught kid skipping class, so kid lied and said teacher hit her. Security camera footage proves teacher's innocence but no consequence for the kid. Not even an apology for the teacher.

A student brought a kitchen knife with a 7-inch blade and threatened an instructional aide with it. Zero punishment.

High school student told two different teachers that he was going to "bang them in the fucking face." Why? He was asked to turn his music off and put his earbuds and phone away at the beginning of the PSAT exam. Absolutely no action was taken, not even a discussion.

Two students stole a teacher's car, but they returned it the next day, so no punishment.

A teacher asked a student to stop talking during a test to which he responded, "Fat ass bitch! Shut the fuck up and lick my balls!" There were zero consequences because he "had unresolved mommy issues and saw the teacher as a mother figure."

A kid jumped on his desk from the floor like a puma and roundhouse kicked a girl in the throat on purpose, with no consequence.

A girl lit the bathroom toilet paper dispenser on fire and had no consequences. Teacher, however, got reamed out in front of her whole class for not watching them closely enough when they go to the bathroom.

A student threw scissors across the room at the teacher and missed her face by an inch or so. No punishment.

A student threatened to kill his teacher. The teacher was told, "As long as he didn't threaten *himself,* we don't care."

A student stole his teacher's cell phone off her desk and smashed it into a million pieces. He bragged about it to other kids, and when the cops confronted him, he stopped coming to school. He never confessed, so the case was closed.

A 6th grader threatened to rape his teacher when she asked him to go back to his seat and redo his assignment neatly. No consequence.

A second grader asked to go to the bathroom but instead, he made a little trip to the front office to steal a coffee mug from the secretary's desk. Next, he barged into a meeting and threw the mug at the principal's head. No consequence.

One kindergartener punched another in the nose for no reason, and they couldn't get it to stop bleeding. He did this two days in a row. No consequence.

A fourth grader brought a knife to school and threatened his teachers with no consequence.

A kid kicked the shit out of his teacher's knee on the second to last day of school and was only suspended the last day because she couldn't walk. She was still in physical therapy months later.

A student stabbed her teacher in the hand with a pen - hard enough to break the skin. The kid told administration that she has "oppositional defiant disorder" and she was sent back to class.

A student wrote a letter to the teacher that said he would burn her house to the ground and then kill her dog and eat it, all for taking away his pen gun that he made in class. There were absolutely zero repercussions for him, and his mother told the teacher that he had every right to speak his mind.

A group of 5th graders looked up porn on their Chromebooks when they were supposed to be researching a planet. The entire class saw the images. The IT department determined that it didn't happen because the search history didn't contain anything like that. (It doesn't take a computer genius to delete the history.)

Kindergarteners engage in chair throwing, table tossing, smacking a teacher, choking each other and leaving marks. Yet these kids are allowed back after getting a lollipop.

A teacher took a student's can of dip and wouldn't return it before the end of the school day. This huge 17-year-old student began banging his head on the window until the window busted. With his nose and forehead bloody, he looked at her and calmly asked, "Can I have it back now?" Because it was deemed a "manifestation of his emotional disability," he was back in his mainstream class the next day.

A student sprayed pepper spray in class, caused three kids to throw up and forced an entire building to be evacuated. No consequence.

A student called the teacher a retard, and a bitch then threw a chair at her. As a result, he got to sit in the office, eat candy, and play games on an iPad for the rest of the day.

Kid broke his teacher's toe with no consequence. A month later the same kid slammed two of the same teacher's fingers in a door. They transferred him to another class, and within a few weeks, his new teacher was on crutches after being pushed down the stairs. *(Why didn't they sue? They could be on a beach sipping those cocktails!)*

Kids openly watched porn in class with the volume all the way up. No consequences.

A kid pushed a teacher down the stairs and broke her spine. No consequence. *(Why didn't she sue? She could be on a beach sipping those cocktails!)*

A kid attempted to strangle her teacher with no consequence. She was back in class a half an hour later with a lollipop and a piece of pizza since she promised she would never do it again.

A student kicked his teacher in her stomach because he didn't want to go to lunch. The teacher was told that the kid was not responsible for his actions because he had emotional problems.

A student stabbed another student in the face with a pencil... like *into* the face... with blood dripping down. No consequence.

A kid peed in his hand and threw it at his teacher. No consequence *(but two thumbs up for creativity!)*

A high school student threatened to kill his teacher and her newborn son as he recited her address to the class and then threw a chair at her. No consequence.

A kid stole $90 from a teacher's purse. He was caught on camera but not punished since he "gave it back."

A student put shit on a shelf in the classroom. He literally pooped in his pants, took it out and ever so gently placed it on a shelf in front of the teacher. No disciplinary action was taken, and they didn't even recommend a mental health evaluation.

A kid punched the teacher in the face on camera. No consequence.

A student made multiple threats against his pregnant teacher. He followed her to her car and pounded on the hood. The principal said, "You must have done something to provoke this, and you need to help him succeed."

A student peed in a cup and dumped the cup on top of the projector and caused it to short circuit. No consequence. *(I mean, who uses that outdated technology anyway?)*

A kid hit two teachers and broke the glass in the office door. He received six hours of free time every day for the rest of the year.

One kid stabbed another kid in the hand with a pencil, and somehow it was the teacher's fault because she "let it happen."

A student intentionally urinated on the classroom floor and then flipped over a piano, smashing it to pieces. No consequence.

A student assaulted another student with a massive literature textbook while the teacher had a substitute. The administration said it was the teacher's fault for "forcing" the students into a new situation (having a sub).

A 3rd grader sent two teachers to the hospital in a one week period, after already assaulting other teachers since he was in kindergarten. Teachers were told it was their fault because they didn't focus 100% of their attention on him 100% of the time. *(Why didn't they sue? They could be on a beach sipping those cocktails!)*

A student put eye drops in a teacher's coffee. When the student was questioned by administration, she said, "I wanted to poison her." They put her in a different class.

A 3rd grader brought a used hypodermic needle to school and poked another girl with it. There was no consequence, not even a phone call home.

A teacher told a kid to slow down in the hallway, he said, "fuck your baby" and punched her in her very pregnant belly. The teacher was told he was new to the school and "needed more time to adjust to the environment."

A girl attempted to sell pot to an aide. When the student was searched hours later, they only found a packed blunt on her that "she only smoked before school." The teacher was told to leave it alone because they were lucky the student comes to school every day.

A kid tried to burn his teacher's face with a cigarette. No consequence.

A student tried to hit his teacher in the head with a 2x4. No consequence.

A student literally hit his teacher several times a day, every day. Over 110 incident reports were made over the course of a year. There was not one thing done ever. Not one. *(I hope that teacher documented everything and lawyered up!)*

A kid told his teacher her breasts were like corn muffins that he wanted to melt in his mouth. No consequence *(but a gold star for creativity!)*

A kid sprayed a teacher with a fire extinguisher. No consequence.

During a teacher's first year a student said in front of the entire class, "I'm getting you a double-headed dildo for Valentine's Day because you need to chill." She told him to leave, and he walked out of the school. Nothing happened after she wrote him up.

A 24-year-old student, just coming from prison for assault and attempted murder, pulled a knife on his teacher and said, "Tell me to sit down again." A student ran to get the principal, but when he showed up, he wanted to know why the teacher had "provoked" the student. They took his knife and sent him to his next class!

Two 7th graders made comic book style drawings of them bending the teacher over a desk, raping her, and then shooting her and putting her body in a garbage bag and throwing it in a dumpster. There was no punishment whatsoever.

A student practically bit a teacher's nipple off and left a scar on her arm after biting her. No consequence.

A first grader trashed the room, and the teacher got in trouble for "making him clean it up" by administration and the parents.

A student filmed under his teacher's dress. No consequence.

A kid brought in "special" brownies and gave them out to his homeroom. The principal laughed and said, "Oh well we can't do anything because they ate all the evidence."

A student stole the principal's credit card and bought stuff online. No consequence.

As outrageous as this all might seem, it is the norm in many schools across the country. Check out these news headlines from 2017-2018[2]:

Are NC schools getting out of control? Fewer teachers feel students behave properly

4J School Board Sets Aside Money to Stop Bad Student Behavior

Disruptive students rattle Medford schools

Buffalo Public Schools address student behavior: teachers complaining about being verbally abused by students

Dallas teachers ask for 'behavior support'

Investigation: In NYC School Where a Teenager Was Killed, Students & Educators Say Lax Discipline Led to Bullying, Chaos, and Death

Where Students Were Stabbed, a School on a Downward Slide

Some D.C. high schools are reporting only a fraction of suspensions

Students attacked, threatened thousands of school employees last year

Seattle Teachers and parents report increase in unruly students

SC teachers face threats and physical harm in the classroom. Many end up quitting

Portland teachers feel classroom environment is unsafe, according to union survey

Texas teacher reveals how disruptive children have forced her to quit her job in viral post - as she shares photos of classroom items 'destroyed' by her students

Hundreds of Akron teachers protest board of education meeting over lack of student discipline by administratin

School bus drivers concerned about discipline, their own safety

Allentown teachers vent to school board: Soft touch approach to discipline backfiring

---

[2] Do I really need to give all the citations for these? If you want to know what newspapers they are from, just google the title! (And don't tell my students I said that!)

At Bakersfield High, students 'cuss up a storm,' fight and assault staff; teachers say new disciplinary practices are to blame

A steady decrease of students disciplined at CT schools

Discipline Policies Complicate Response to Violent Episodes at Lincoln High

Behavior in high schools declines amid changes in society, discipline policies

Teachers claim discipline crisis at Paso Robles Joint Unified School District

MUSD's Discipline Crisis reaches Boiling Point

S.C. Study Finds Student Discipline Issues Prompt Teacher Turnover

Suffolk teachers blast administration for creating unsafe environment

Parents' concerns growing over reported violence, lack of discipline at Pinellas School

Does Broward Schools' Program Coddle Troubled Students and Excuse Dangerous Behavior?

Youngstown teacher fed up with bad behavior going unchecked

Beaumont Middle School adds security guard after parents complain of violence, brawls

New Mexico struggling to keep schools filled with teachers due to lack of discipline

Tulsa Public Schools loses 35 percent of its teachers in two years, but many aren't leaving for higher pay (cites discipline as #1 issue)

Dorchester BOE hears concerns about teachers leaving (cites discipline as #1 issue)

Louisiana's teacher shortage is real; here's what caused it, how state lawmakers look to solve it (cites discipline as #1 issue)

Undisciplined: Chaos may be coming to Minnesota classrooms, by decree

When Students Assault Teachers, Effects Linger

Fighting Poverty, Drugs and Even Violence, All on a Teacher's Salary

Parents Say Scope of Bullying Hidden

Teacher: We Didn't Sign Up for This

Fewer Suspensions, More 'Hugs and Bubbles': Oklahoma City's Experiment in School Discipline

Minnesota Teacher: "We're Powerless to Discipline"

Baltimore County teachers protest discipline problems in schools

Madison school discipline is a hot mess

Letter: Discipline, morale real problems in school

Suspension Reform Is Tormenting Schools

When school-discipline 'reform' makes schools less safe

To be clear, I understand that this is a complicated issue that involves many factors, discrimination being the main one. This matter obviously needs to be looked into on a much deeper level. However, completely abandoning discipline policies in lieu of chats and writing assignments (which often do not happen anyway) is not the answer either. This sends a strong message to the students that they can pretty much do whatever they want with no consequence. But throwing kids out for days, weeks, or even permanently is not helping that student (though it does give the teacher and other students a welcome break). If the powers that be really wanted to "stop the school to prison pipeline" and help troubled kids, they would invest much more money into our schools or pay more attention to where they currently invest it.[3] With

---

[3] For example, in 2010 Pearson received $186 million to write the shitty PARCC test. By 2018, only 5 states were using it, and by my estimation, soon it will be none.

more funding, schools could handle larger amounts of in-school suspensions and have teachers and tutors run them. They could hire many more counselors and psychologists (as opposed to ONE for a school of 3,000 kids). They could pay teachers adequately for supervising detention (for now, they generally make the teacher hold a student in their own room, for no extra pay). A secretary could be hired to keep track of detentions and in-school suspensions. More therapeutic programs could be created for students with mental health problems. Perhaps, with enough funding and effort, the idea of restorative justice might actually work. But completely removing discipline from schools and replacing it with a nice idea is only making schools uncontrollable and unsafe.

27

EATING THE CAKE

"They say you can't have cake and eat it too. Ain't you s'posed
to eat it too?"
-Trey Songz

I suppose every generation thinks the next one is moving too fast with their sexuality. When I was in middle school in the mid 90's, we were just getting into making out, and the few kids who did more than that were anomalies (or heroes to some). Sex was something you experimented with in your later high school years, if not in college. If you had asked me then how much more advanced the kids of the future would be, I wouldn't have really had an answer. Sex in high school seems as advanced as it gets. I mean, a lot of them aren't even finished with puberty in middle school, so what exactly are they doing?

They're doing all of it and more if you believe what they say. Statistics show that the average age at which a teenager loses their virginity is between 16 and 17. But just because they haven't had sex in the traditional way doesn't mean they aren't doing some pretty mature things. The internet changed the way that kids learn about sex. It used to be whispered about between friends. Occasionally a kid stole a porn magazine or VHS tape from his parents, and that was the thing that educated a whole neighborhood of kids. But otherwise, kids were left with rumors, encyclopedias, the maturation talk in elementary school, and a chat with mom or dad (if you could handle the embarrassment). Kids now have access to porn from the youngest of ages. Even parents who keep a tight lock on their kid's internet and phone usage cannot control what the other kids have available. They see the most extreme sexual situations between people who are professional actors (okay, not really *actors*, more like professionally trained fornicators) and thinking it is normal.

Take, for example, analingus. This is something that was mostly considered taboo until recently. It wasn't a thing you heard about often, and it certainly wasn't spoken about in popular song lyrics. Whatever goes on between two consenting adults in the privacy of their own dwelling is one thing. What is weirding me out is how normal this act seems to be with young people.

I hear them talk about it like a friendly gesture, a mere kiss on the cheek. And it's in lots of mainstream songs. That's how all this butt stuff became conventional in the first place- music. "The origins of the current booty-eating moment—at least within hip-hop culture—can be traced to a series of interviews with Louisiana-rapper Kevin Gates. In an interview along with DJ Whoo Kid,

Gates responded to a question about groupie love by saying, 'I'm passionate about whatever woman that I'm making love to at the time- I'm supposed to eat all yo' booty. This how I'm living.' The interview then morphs into a conversation strictly about tossing salad, with Whoo Kid chiming in that he, too, has been known to eat booty."[62]

Apparently, this interview went viral across social media and made Gates much more popular. He then uttered his infamous quote in another interview, "Yeah I eat booty! Real n****s eat booty! Real n****s please they bitches!" Miami rapper Trick Daddy followed suit by declaring August 5th National Eat-A-Booty Day. The internet exploded with parodies, memes and endless discussions on the topic of licking butts.

Then male hip-hop stars started to take this topic very seriously. Female hip hop artists had been mentioning this topic for a few years (Lil Kim with "He be lookin kinda fruity, but he still could lick the booty," Khia raps, "lick my pussy and my crack," and Nicki Minaj penned, "Somebody point me to the best ass eater.") And suddenly it was more acceptable for men to want this too. Rapper Ghostface Killah says, "We eat fish, toss salads, and make rap ballads," Action Bronson raps, "Couple of months you probably see me with an actress/Getting my ass licked." Other hip-hop artists who mention butt licking in their songs include Lil Wayne, Tyler, the Creator, Sean Price, Gucci Mane, Kevin Gates and a whole bunch of other guys I've never heard of.[63]

Next, mainstream magazines started publishing serious articles on the matter. In 2013, Playboy released an article entitled, "The Men Who Want This Sex Act Aren't Kidding," Cosmo followed with a how-to guide ("If you are performing analingus on a hairy guy, just part the hair with your hands")[64], Salon tried to explain "Why Analingus is on the Rise," Ebony and GQ magazine released guides for this practice and Complex magazine released an article called, "You're Doing it Wrong: Tossing Salad" which included tips such as, "Don't forget to trim and don't forget to come up for air."[65] (Do you really need that tip? Has anyone ever suffocated during this act?)

And then references to butt stuff started appearing in mainstream songs. The song "Post to Be" by Omarion ft. Chris Brown contains the now infamous line, "But he gotta eat the booty like groceries." Ask any high school teacher, and they'll tell you they've heard this uttered in the classroom at least 3 times. Once I learned that "cake" is a slang term for a big ass, I started to notice how many popular songs were talking about analingus. Artist Trey Songz has a song called "Cake" where he says, "They say you can't have cake and eat it too. Ain't you s'posed to eat it too? I just wanna taste, once I blow the candles out, put it in my face." Rihanna has a song called "Birthday Cake" about wanting her butt enjoyed for her birthday. And the group DNCE has that seemingly innocent song "Cake by the Ocean," which you couldn't escape during the summer of 2017. Replace the word "cake" with "butt" and think about those lyrics. "See you licking frosting from your own hands, Want another taste, I'm begging… I'm going blind from this sweet, sweet craving, I keep on hoping we'll eat BUTT (cake) by the ocean, you're fucking delicious." A little weird listening to that song with your kids now, huh?

My whole point in bringing this up is that I'm totally shocked by what has become normal for teens. What adults do is one thing, but are these kids seriously doing this act *casually*? That seems like a really bad idea, for so many reasons. I'll let you use your imagination.

And then there's the issue of squirting. There is much debate about whether or not this is even real. Some people claim that females can actually ejaculate a fluid, while others maintain that the fluid is urine and that "female ejaculation" is merely sexy urination. Whatever it is, it isn't easy to achieve, and for some people, it is becoming the hallmark of a good sexual experience. In his song entitled "Squirt," rapper Lil B says, "I like when you squirt, I'm gon' work, she gon' squirt," and he goes on to talk about all of the strenuous things he is going to have to engage in to get this "bitch" to squirt (The chorus of the song literally repeats the line "Make that bitch squirt" 16 times). So obviously if the female does not produce a liquid of sorts, Lil B did not complete his mission. Imagine the pressure this now puts on females (the ones who buy into this shit) to *prove* their satisfaction. I remember the desperate need I felt in high school to keep my boyfriend happy in that way (never really considering what might make *me* happy but that's another book entirely) and I can't even imagine having to figure out how to ejaculate just to stroke his ego. I have a feeling a lot of girls are giving themselves urinary tract infections and a lot of teens are unknowingly peeing on each other.

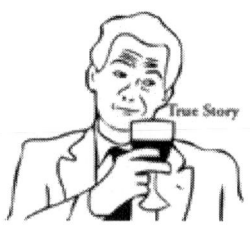

I asked a few sex ed. teachers to share with me the weirdest/dumbest questions they've gotten from students (I fixed the spelling and grammar for the sake of readability). The students are often allowed to anonymously write down their queries for the teacher to answer in front of the class. Here is a list of those questions with the hypothetical answers I would give (which is probably why it's a good thing I don't teach sex ed.):

How do I get rid of fungus on my balls?

I think the more important question is why you have fungus on your balls in the first place!

What kind of energy do guys get when they're in heat?

Gravitational.

Why do females chew on your balls?

Because they hate you.

What do I do when my girl wants me to put my whole arm in?

Run.

If I have sperm on my hand and touch the doorknob, then my mom touches the doorknob and touches herself, can she get pregnant?

Maybe you should just try to avoid that situation by washing your hands?

If I'm in a hot tub with fifty guys and they all ejaculate, can I get pregnant?

Eww. Why… how… why… just… YES.

If you're having anal sex with a girl and she farts, will your balls explode?

Probably.

Does cum make your hair softer?

Whoever told you that is lying.

Do twins happen because of a threesome?

Sometimes.

Isn't there any way that the boy can have the baby?

Not yet, but we need to find a way!

If a pregnant lady takes a bath will the baby drown?

Not if she keeps her legs closed.

What do I do if I swallow the used condom?

Rejoice.

Do they make chicken flavored condoms?

I don't know, but they should!

When I shake it there's a little pain. Is it bad?

Stop shaking it.

What is a punanie?

Google it.

If a white man has sex with a black woman and then has sex with a white woman can the white woman have a black baby?

Maybe.

What is a blue waffle?

Google image search it, if you dare.

How do you stretch a guy's booty hole?

Gently.

Where do boys put tampons?

Wherever they want!

Can you keep sperm in a jar like pets in a fish tank?

Sort of.

If gay guys like things in their butt do they get turned on when they poop?

These are the things you think about?

Do steroids give your penis muscles?

Yes, and the ladies love it.

Is it true if you eat eggs your period will stink?

Not if they're free range.

If you blow into the penis will your balls inflate like a balloon?

The research is inconclusive.

What's a wolf pussy?

What they all looked like before the year 2000.

Can the dick go in other holes like ear, eye, and nose?

Not usually.

Can a dog wear a condom?

Technically yes.

Can you use a skittles bag as a condom?

Don't count on it.

If she farts on your penis will it pop or bleed?

Why is she farting on your penis though (#nojudgment)?

Is it true if you put lemon on your penis and it burns you have a disease?

Possibly.

What is a mangina?

I'm not entirely sure but I like the sound of it.

Does a lady fart when she's going to have a baby?

More like *while* she's having the baby. It's not like an alarm system that happens beforehand.

Can you get someone's butt pregnant?

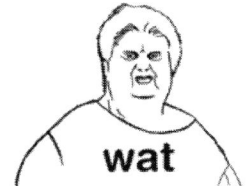

Why do some girls have a penis?

It's complicated.
If sperms have tails why don't we?

I've always wondered that!
Do you put the balls in too?

You can certainly try!
Would a plastic bag work as a condom?

Outlook not so good.
Is it normal to have one very long pube?

Not really, but it's interesting.
What's an Alaskan pipeline?

I'm too afraid to find out.

28

TEENAGERS SAY THE DARNDEST FUCKING THINGS

"Miss, you're so chill, I can't even tell when you're on your period!"
-Student

The following are real conversations that happened in the classroom:

Teacher: "Take it from me, you're going to want to pay attention to this."

Student: "Your mom took it from me!"

Student: "Miss, can I ask you a question about college?"

Teacher: "Sure."

Student: "Did you ever have a threesome?"

Teacher: "Did you really just ask me that?"

Student: "No."

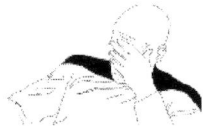

Student: "Can I borrow $5?"

Teacher: "I don't have any money."

Student: "You should become a stripper. You don't have to pay taxes and you would make more money than being a teacher. Plus, I'd pay to see that."

Teacher: "Not if you don't even have $5. Now get away from me."

Student: "Do you have any kids?"

Teacher: "Nope."

Student *(with a creepy wink):* "I could help you fix that!"

Teacher: "I'm not interested in adopting you."

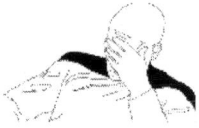

Student 1: "Miss, did you do anything fun for your birthday?"

Student 2: "She looks like the kind of lady that hits up a strip club and makes it rain."

Student 1:"Nah, man... she's a *teacher*. She can only make it hail fuckin pennies and shit!"

Student 1: "I just don't understand anything you're talking about!"

Teacher: "I'd be happy to tutor you any time before or after school.

Student 2 *(while making obscene gestures):* "I'll let you tutor me... in human anatomy!"

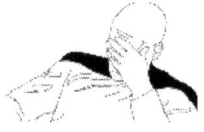

Student 1: "Just do it bro! You're such a pussy!"

Teacher: "Please don't use that language. I really don't like that word."

Student 1: "Why do you care miss? You got one! You should be proud!"

Student 1: "I don't even know what half of the words mean."

Teacher: "Well, it starts with I pledge allegiance to the flag, which means-"

Student 2: "I pledge allegiance to that ass!"

Student 1: "What's partition mean?"

Teacher: "It means divided into parts."

Student 2: "No, you're using the word wrong cause a partition is a tryout for prostitutes. It's in that Beyoncé song!"

Student 1: "So onomatopoeia is, like, a word that's supposed to be, like, a sound?"

Teacher: "Somewhat, yes. Like boom or woof."

Student 2: Or SKEET SKEET SKEET SKEET SKEET!"[66]

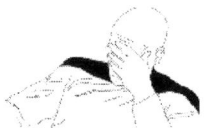

Teacher: "Are there any questions?"

Student: "Have you ever had blonde hair because I watched a porn last night and the girl that was getting banged from behind looked just like you!"

Teacher: "Well then… Does anyone have any questions about the *Battle of Gettysburg?*"

Student 1: "What's the test going to be like?"

Teacher: "Long and hard!"

Student 2: "That's what she said!"

Teacher: "I guess I walked right into that one."

Student 3: "Ya kinda did."

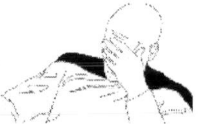

Student: "Do you like Wendy's?"

Teacher: "Yeah it's okay. Why?"

Student: "I think you'll like it *when-deez* nuts are in your mouth!"

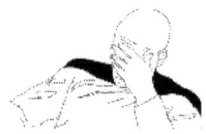

Teacher: "At the time, Dick Cheney was the vice president."

Student 1: "Is that his real name?"

Teacher: "Dick is a nickname for Richard."

Student 2: "When I grow up I am going to name my son Richard. And when he gets in trouble at school, I am going to go home and beat my Dick!"

Teacher: "When I was your age, there was no internet or social media. We had to look things up in books."

Student 1: "How did you look at porn!?"

Student: "Wanna hear a joke?!"

Teacher: "Sure!"

Student: "If I was a baker, and you were a donut - I'd fill you with cream!"

Teacher: "Please stop making that noise."

Student: "You didn't say that last night!"

Teacher: "I'm going to be out tomorrow for medical tests."

Student: "What's wrong Miss? Do you have herpes?"

Student: "You wanna go to prom with me?"

Teacher: "I have a wife, and I'm your teacher so, no."

Student: "She don't gotta know."

Teacher: "What will your parents say when I tell them you said this?"

Student: "I don't know. I don't live with them. I got my own apartment. You should come over."

Teacher: "Yes? Do you need help?"

Student: "No, I just called you over here so I could watch you walk away."

(Teacher is wearing Harvard shirt)

Student 1: "Did you really go to Harvard?"

Student 2: "Of course she didn't go to Harvard! *She's a teacher!*"

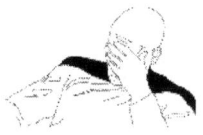

Student: "So like Queen Elizabeth has been a queen since Shakespeare was alive? I didn't know people could live 400 years."

Student: "Like why didn't Daisy just text Gatsby when she got home?"

Student: "Can I read you my thesis, and you tell me if it's good?"

Teacher: "Sure, go ahead."

Student: "The government should not force people to vaccinate their kids because I got all those shots and I never got any of those diseases, so that shows that it doesn't matter."

Teacher: "That doesn't make sense. You *didn't* get those diseases because you *were* vaccinated."

Student: "Oh. Wait, no! You don't need them because I never got sick!"

Teacher: "You never got sick because you got the shots!"

Student: "But the government shouldn't make people get shots because you never even hear about people getting those kind of things anymore. I've never heard of anyone with polio!"

Teacher: "You don't hear about those diseases anymore because most people get vaccinated. Do you understand?"

Student: "Umm, yeah."

Teacher: "You need to fix your thesis."

Student: "Okay."

5 minutes later student hands teacher a paper that says, "The government should not force people to vaccinate their kids because everyone got those shots and those diseases aren't here anymore, so that shows that it doesn't matter."

Teacher: "Anyone remember who painted the Mona Lisa?"

Student: "Leonardo DiCaprio."

Student: "What's the name of the person in the play we been reading about?"

Teacher: "Julius Caesar."

Student: "That's a girl, right?"

Teacher: "No."

Student: "Is he still alive?"

Teacher: "Chivalry is dead!"

Student: "Who is Chivalry? Is that a new student?"

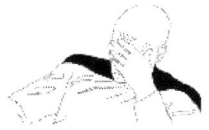

Class is talking about Pearl Harbor

Student: "Wait! I remember her! What did she do again?"

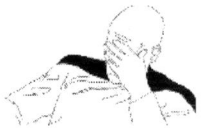

Student: "If you're telling us sperm cells contain glucose, which is a sugar, then why does it taste so salty?!"

Here are some other gems that have been said to teachers across the country:

"Miss you thick! It looks like you have a diaper on."

"If you lost a little weight I would ask you to the school dance."

"We should put you on eBay to find you a husband!"

"You're getting fluffy. You need to come to my dad's gym!"

"Are you a computer? Because you turn my floppy disk into a hard drive."

"My Grandma says you're a moron."

"Do you ever put your finger in your husband's butt?"

"What does semen taste like?"

"Your room smells like lip smackers and dildos."

"I put axe shower gel on my balls, and it burned."

"You dress different than the other teachers like you want a baby put in you."

"Miss, I ain't got no belt on, so if my dick falls out, it's my bad.

29

TEACHER COMMENTS AND WHAT THEY REALLY MEAN

"When I was a kid, a teacher's salary was a middle-class salary. Teachers knew the community was going to cover them. And they knew they would have the summer off. People just don't fucking get it. It's not just an eight-hour job. Any really good teacher is in there ten, twelve, fourteen hours a day. They're grading papers that most of you who fucking bitch about teaching, couldn't sit down and get through three of them. 'Oh, but they get the summer off.' Fuck you. If you didn't give the teacher their summer off, you fucking moron... Are you shitting me? I tell you, we'd have to be building insane asylums to the sky."

Lewis Black

Inquisitive/enthusiastic/eager = *annoying*

Learning begins at home = *now that I have met you, I see why your kid is the way he is*

Have you considered making hygiene a part of his daily routine? = *Your kid stinks*

It's been an interesting semester = *your kid is one of the most difficult I've had in years*

Always smiling = *because he has no idea what's going on*

Great language skills/enjoys spending time with friends/active participant in discussions = *won't shut up*

Has many insightful ideas to share with the class/class leader = *bossy*

Problem solves independently = *can tie her own shoes*

Behavior can be a bit unpredictable = *farts a lot*

Follows directions/turns work in on time/uses class time constructively = *One of six kids in class with a similar name so I can't really remember who he is right now*

Works better independently rather than in a group setting = *when we put her in a group she loses her mind*

Sensitive = *crybaby*

Shows commitment to school = *could be absent a bit more*

Lacks focus/easily distracted = *If a bug flies by the window, your kid is lost for hours*

Attitude needs improvement = *Says "I hate you" on a daily basis*

Learning how to be a better listener = *Asks what we are doing after I explained the directions five times in a row*

Has a mature vocabulary = *Says "fuck" a lot*

30

LETTER TO MY STUDENTS

"The lesson of report cards, grades, and tests is that children should not trust themselves or their parents but should instead rely on the evaluation of certified officials. People need to be told what they are worth."
-John Taylor Gatto

Yeah, there *are* some good kids. There are wonderful, sensitive, thoughtful, kind kids who give me back a bit of faith in humanity. Unfortunately, in my experience, these kids are way too hard on themselves. While teachers are doing everything we can think of to get some kids to care about their future, these kids hear the message loud and clear and translate it into anxiety and fear. We apply so much pressure to kids these days, as though every test and every decision in high school makes or breaks their entire future. And while it has no effect on many, it sends the wrong message to the ones who are really listening. After a few years of having the same pep talk with my classes, I decided to write down my thoughts and hand it out instead. Perhaps you might want to share this with your students or kids.

Dear students,

Every year the guidance counselors come into my classroom to give a presentation to my 11th graders. For about 45 minutes they talk about standardized test scores, college applications, GPA, class rank, etc. By the time they leave, most students are on the verge of having an anxiety attack, and who could blame them? They have just been fed the terrifying idea that any possibility of future success all depends on what they have accomplished up until that point, and how they will convey those accomplishments to colleges. Students are also made to feel that they have to choose what they want to do for the rest of their lives within the next year or two.

They are not the only ones filled with anxiety. So many stories are racing through my mind, and I feel the responsibility to tell the students the truth. The lecture I end up giving is exhausting, so I decided to try to write it down. But where to begin?

Let me start by saying that *in no way does what you have done in high school have to determine how successful you will be, how much money you will make or how happy you will be as an adult.* Can it? Sure. Lots of students excel in school and go on to very successful college careers and rewarding jobs. But many others do not do well in school because of their home life, the absence of maturity, lack of a good public school education or anything else, yet still they go on to have a successful adult life.

Take my brother, for example. He is very smart and has a quick mind. He is excellent at leading a team and arguing a point. He can easily excel at academics if he chooses to. But in high school he didn't care, because he couldn't see how school was a path to get to where he wanted to be. Besides, he was the lead singer of a band that was going to make it.

The band broke up. He went to a state school for one semester and dropped out. He was lost. He had no idea what he was passionate about. He worked a few retail jobs and went to community college where he was lucky enough to have professors who saw the enormous potential in him and pushed him to excel. He got straight A's and transferred to a highly ranked university to study philosophy. Our family was adamantly against this. They thought it was an unrealistic and useless thing to major in. My brother chose to study what he loved and graduated at the top of his class. Then he went to a prestigious law school to study international law, and eventually landed a job at one of the nation's leading law firms. Any of his teachers from high school would have been surprised by his success. He showed no signs of this back then. But then again, no one really tried to see past how he presented himself to the world.

You don't have to be good at academics to be successful. My best friend never did well in school and hated it. She went to many different colleges, off and on, for years, and never graduated. She was always interested in fashion and had a unique style. She started to volunteer to help with various fashion shoots and runway shows and eventually she developed a reputation and online following. Then she got paying jobs that sent her all over the world to style photo shoots. She is now the lead stylist for a luxury department store where I can't afford a pair of socks. She makes three times as much money as me, and I have a Master's degree from one of the top ten universities in the country. (Her husband is a graphic designer who makes four times as much money as me with only a community college education.)

There are also many people who dedicate their whole lives to doing well in school, but it doesn't matter in the end. The valedictorian of my graduating high school class got full scholarships to wherever he wanted to go. He studied music (his passion) and became a music teacher. He was laid off and couldn't get another job. He is now a very unhappy travel agent.

A friend of mine from high school went to a very distinguished university and graduated with over $120,000 in loans. She became a school psychologist, and most of her paycheck goes towards paying those loans. She likes her job but could have gotten the same degree for a fraction of the price.

I hope that these examples illustrate the diverse nature of success in our society and the countless roads that can get you there. It is often less about grades, and more about hard work, determination, and creativity. After you graduate high school, no one will ever ask you for your SAT scores or what your GPA was. I cannot even remember what I got on the SAT, but I know it wasn't noteworthy. *Don't let anyone make you feel that your options are limited because of the past. Every day is a new opportunity to completely redesign your life. I really believe this.*

And please, for the love of god, *don't try to figure out what you will do with the rest of your life right now!* How could anyone know what they will want to do as an adult at 17 years old? That is absurd. Just follow your passion and the road will lead you where you are meant to go. Take the subject or topic that is the most exciting, the easiest or most exciting and take more of those classes! The path will reveal itself.

Don't get me wrong. School is important. I'm a teacher. *Obviously* I feel that way. But you can still take advantage of educational opportunities at any time in your life, and every school has opportunities that can lead to where you want to be.

So relax. If you don't have any idea what you are doing right now, that is completely normal! *Okay?*

31

IT DOESN'T HAVE TO BE THIS WAY

"It is a miracle that curiosity survives

formal education."

Albert Einstein

It's so complicated. Students are not paying attention because they're bored. They're bored because what's on their phone will always be more entertaining than anything I have to offer them.

On the one hand, I feel that not everything has to be entertaining for you to care about it. I am not here to entertain you. I am here to *teach* you, and you need to do what you're *supposed* to do sometimes, not just what you *want* to do. On the other hand, I understand why they're bored because I am also bored. *This is not why I became a teacher.*

I did not become a teacher to force kids to do stupid meaningless tasks that do not require any critical thinking, creativity or any real skill other than spitting back out exactly what I tell them to spit out. I became a teacher to make kids think deeply about every aspect of life. And to me, there's no better way to do that than through examining literature. But the curriculum and the standards and the testing has really sucked the joy out of it. The job is hard enough without a useless curriculum.

Every year they're paying more attention to whether or not we are following the script. They give us less and less room for creativity. We rarely get to generate our own lessons or choose our own books. And it really feels like they don't trust us. I am feeling more and more like a babysitter. I don't enjoy assigning (or reading) an essay that I think is a waste of time. I do not like having to train a kid to write an essay that is clearly a waste of their time and then having to rip it apart completely. Neither of us gives a shit about it. And these are not skills that any of these students are going to be able to use, even in college. I majored in English and never once did I have to analyze the structure or literary elements within a text. I'm pretty sure that no other major or job would require that either.

Teachers are passionate people (or we used to be). That's why we went into this profession. I'm sure that most of us had no idea how difficult it would be. We couldn't foresee all the changes in technology and how much more challenging it would make the job. But we truly care about the subjects that we teach. We see the value in them, and we want to make it easier for students to appreciate and pass our passion on to them. If "they" would trust us to create our own lessons and choose our own materials, the flame would be reignited!

And when students see that a teacher truly loves and is genuinely interested in what they're teaching, they start to care about it too. Every time I teach a book or lesson that's truly important to me, something I had a hand in crafting myself, many kids actually put down their phones of their own accord. They can't help but tune in to what I'm saying because they feel that it's worth paying attention to. They want to know what I am so excited about.

But instead, we're all kind of miserable. We're trapped in this place where so much of what we do is a waste of time, and it's not going to get any better until this country and the powers that be start to trust their teachers. They must trust that *nobody* would stay in this job longer than a year or two unless they really cared about the students and the subject matter. But they never ask us what we think. Or if they *do* ask us what we think, they do absolutely nothing with that information. It's almost like an exercise to make us *feel better*, to give us the illusion that we're being listened to. But we all know that our opinions and ideas almost never get taken into consideration which makes absolutely no sense. In any other situation, you would ask the person who does the task every day how it can be improved. If I wanted to know how to milk a cow, I wouldn't ask someone who has studied how to milk a cow but has never actually done it. I would go straight to the source.

It is such a complicated situation in education right now. We are living in a time where life and technology are more exciting than they have ever been. But life and work can't always be thrilling and interesting and completely stimulating and entertaining. And kids *do* need to learn that in life you just have to do things sometimes that don't entertain you because that's part of the deal. A good portion of adult life is doing things you don't want to do in order to have the things you want to have. But students are not adults yet. They shouldn't be doing things all day long that are boring, pointless and completely unrelated to their lives. That's not what education is for. The kids have shut off, and a lot of us have shut off too. It could be so different. It doesn't have to be this way. But until people put a little trust in teachers, it's only going to get worse.

32

"YOU'RE TOO TALL" AND OTHER AREAS FOR IMPROVEMENT

"You're too tall. It might be intimidating to some of the kids."

-A comment on a teacher's formal evaluation

Teachers get mistreated and downright abused by students and parents. There isn't a whole lot we can do to change that until society changes its perception of teachers. A much bigger problem with an obvious answer is administrators who treat teachers and other school employees like goat shit. When they observe us for our evaluations, they often write the pettiest, ridiculous, and meaningless things. We are also "written up" for equally petty reasons, which results in a "letter" being put in our "file." If these "letters" start to become excessive, they can initiate the process to get rid of you.

Administrators can change how society is *allowed* to treat us. They can't stop them from treating us inappropriately, but they can have very clear consequences for students and even parents. They often promise there will be consequences, but they rarely follow through on those promises. They give society the message that YES, throwing a fit and treating people with disrespect is indeed an effective way to solve your problems or cope with your own life. If they followed through more often, students would understand that disrespecting teachers will not be tolerated. As far as parents, they can stop kissing their asses and tell them that cursing out a teacher will also not be tolerated. They are welcome to come back when they are ready to handle the problem like an adult. But when administrators give "write-ups" to teachers and ding them on their evaluations for extremely stupid reasons, they set a precedent for everyone else. Their message is obvious: it is perfectly okay to treat teachers like garbage.

The following are real comments that were written on teachers' formal evaluations:

"You're overzealous and too friendly."

"Your sink isn't clean." (In an art class that was painting.)

"You have a lot of absent students during 1st period. What are your plans to improve their attendance?"

"Your classroom needs cuter curtains."

"You should say 'yes' instead of 'yup' when responding to students' questions."

"Your carpet is dirty." (Kindergarten class)

"You're too positive."

"We just love your quirky little self."

"You didn't say 'in conclusion' so students didn't know you were wrapping up the lesson."

"You didn't get all the kids' names right!" (It was 3rd day of school.)

"Your classroom is too bare." (Teacher shares five different classrooms and transports materials on a cart.)

"You did not fill out an incident report in the mandatory 24-hour window." (Teacher had her nose broken.)

"You say 'good job' too much."

"You did too well in this area, so I'm giving you a satisfactory rating instead of exceeds expectations."

"You really shouldn't put the popsicle sticks somewhere they could fall."

"You're too nurturing."

"Too many kids had to sharpen their pencils."

"Your voice is naturally too loud for a calming learning environment."

"You say 'guys' too much."

"You need a college corner." (It was directly behind her.)

"Have you ever considered vocal modulation lessons because the sound of your high pitched voice is driving your students crazy."

"I would give you a perfect score, amazing lesson, but I just won't give out perfect scores."

"You smile too much."

"You corrected their grammar." (She's an English teacher.)

"Your use of technology is below average." (All he had in his room was a school-issued overhead projector.)

"You called on more boys than girls." (There were only 4 girls in the class.)

"A student blew her nose for over one minute. That is instructional time that is wasted."

"Write your objective on the left side of the board, not the right. I prefer the left."

"You're tall. It may be intimidating to the kids."

"You're too loud."

"You take your position too seriously and don't give students a break — build better bridges/relationships with parents and students. Cut them slack when they aren't trying stuff. Our students have a lot going on and need friends."

"I know you're a female and all, but you need to be less emotional."

"You wore pants to conferences; most other teachers wear dresses."

"Should try having students solve a word problem or two during small group." (Elementary general music class)

"Your expectations are too high."

"I know you were talking to a student in a 'crisis,' but you really need to be in the hallway during transitions."

"Your classroom is too small and looks cramped!" (Classroom used to be a small office and was issued to her by the same administrator.)

"Your whiteboards are dirty."

"Your problem is that during assemblies, you sit angry. No one likes you because of it."

"You're too nice. The students take it as weakness."

"You need to sharpen the kids' pencils for them daily because it was wasting learning time for them to sharpen them themselves."

"Your clothes are too tight."

"It's too cold in your room, and the kids can't focus."(Teacher taught in a room with a huge hole in the window. It was the middle of winter. When she asked when they would fix it she was instructed to fix it herself by putting Saran Wrap over the hole.)

"You need to find somewhere else to keep your jacket." (Teacher kept his jacket on the back of his chair because there were no closets, hooks or even doors.)

"You used the word 'thing' when teaching."

"You are too professional."

"I couldn't understand you because you spoke Spanish the whole time." (It was Spanish class.)

Administrator stops teacher during the beginning of observation and says, "That shelf is unsafe, and it needs to come down." The teacher nodded and kept teaching. Administrator says, "No, *now*. Take all of your things off there. The whole class sat and watched as she had to shamefully take dozens of books off the shelf.

"You don't seem to have rapport with your students, probably because you don't have children of your own."

"Classroom smelled like nail polish." (It was the cheap dry erase markers they had given the teachers at the beginning of the school year.)

"You said 'should' too much."

"Don't call your students ladies and gentlemen. It's too respectful."

"You should wear a more supportive bra."

"You have too good of a connection with your students."

"Walk with more purpose."

"You have too many trash cans in your room."

"You go above and beyond when I just need you to throw what I ask you to do together, and not make it picture perfect. Also, you accessed your work email during off hours on your mobile, so I'll have to write you up for that."

"You did well in the lesson, but since you're a new teacher, I'm going to rate you basic. All new teacher get basic."

"Your curtains are ugly, take them down."

"You used please and thank you too much during your lesson."

"Sometimes your voice reaches tones that make you sound babyish. I suggest you record your voice and listen to when that happens and correct it."

"There are three blueberries on the floor."

"The chairs are uncomfortable."

"Your PowerPoint has too much green in it."

"You really need to dust the insides of the empty desks in your classroom."

"Your AC is running too loud."

"Smile more with your eyes!"

"You are clearly a good teacher you just need to fine-tune some aspects of your teaching. You're like a Cadillac with bald tires."

"You weren't motherly enough." (High school class)

"The rug isn't centered symmetrically in front of your smart board."

"You move around too much when you're talking."

"You need to.be more enthusiastic." (Teacher was 39 weeks pregnant.)

"You didn't address Brittany's question during the lesson." (There was no student named Brittany in the class.)

"You're not a shitty teacher."

"There were papers on the table."

"Your lesson isn't unsatisfactory I just didn't like it."

"You are like the fluff on the top of a milkshake. When you see a milkshake, it looks full and substantial, but then you realize there is just fluff at the top that is all air. You are like the fluff."

"Your outfit was intimidating because it looked expensive."

"The broom wasn't all the way behind the classroom door."

"The way you look is distracting to students. Try wearing more muted colors."

'That student was coughing too much; you should have made her go to the nurse."

"Your kids are having too much fun in your class. There is no way they are learning."

"You must carry your lesson plan in your hands at all times. You cannot put it down."

"You are too dependent on the textbook." (The class didn't use a textbook.)

"A child picked his nose for the duration of the class. You taught through it and didn't stop to have the child wash his hands."

"You shouldn't say that the students are 'done.' A turkey is done, students are 'finished.' "

"You should probably quit teaching and move on to another career."

"Carry a clipboard and pretend to write about the kids on it. It will intimidate them, and they will behave."

"You are only proficient (not distinguished) because you are monitoring and correcting student behaviors. Students need to take more responsibility for their learning. They need to protect instructional time by disciplining each other." (They were 6th graders.)

"You used the word 'caveat.' That word is too advanced for your class." (It was an 11th grade English class.)

"You are too enthusiastic."

"It took 72 seconds for you to hand out and explain the next activity to 32 students. That is way too long."

"I can tell you put a lot of effort into your lessons. But you really shouldn't be doing that much work."

"The stack of chairs in your classroom is not welcoming."

"You wasted instructional time by saying 'raise your hand.'

"Your class should be like Miss Frizzle's class." (You got a magic school bus in this bitch?)

"You didn't explain to the children that Pluto is not a planet anymore while teaching the planets." (The teacher discussed this while the administrator talked on her phone during the class.)

"I don't like the font that you chose to write your lesson plans in."

"Why are the students wearing coats? Unacceptable!" (It was February and the heat was broken."

"You say 'okay' too much."

"You've lost your sparkle."

"Your classroom is too colorful. It's almost cold and uninviting."

"I don't really know what you do, but you appear to do it well."

"You drank too much water during your lesson."

"You looked tired and kept rubbing your eyes. I hope you aren't getting the flu that's going around." (That was the entirety of the comment section on the evaluation form.)

"I'm worried you are letting your anal-ness take over your teaching."

"The purple on the bulletin boards is too purple."

"You should teach in a private school because you believe in the kids too much."

"Student asked for a ruler. You did not have one. You were unprepared." (It was a high school English class.)

"You blow your whistle too hard!" (It was a gym class.)

"I didn't like the way you took off your cardigan."

"I just wasn't inspired. I could tell the students were, but I wasn't."

"The temperature in your room is too warm." (The temperature is controlled by a company in another state.)

"I don't like the way you sit. I don't like the way you stand."

"You're a cupcake, and you need to be more like an avocado."

"I feel you have a poor classroom culture because one student answered without raising his hand. I know you listed modifications for him as he is labeled ED but that was disrespectful."

"Your sartorial splendor is beyond reproach."

"Your bulletin board doesn't have a border."

"Your students are too quiet."

"The door was open when I arrived. It should be closed during class."

"Your boards were too chalky."

"Your personal life seems to be affecting your job." (Teacher took two days off two weeks prior to evaluation because her marriage had just ended.)

"You shouldn't keep your water bottle on your table during small group instruction."

"Your windows were open too wide."

"Your kids are reading, and they shouldn't be doing that in class."

"Your classroom plant could use some water."

"Use smartboard." (There was no smartboard.)

"You couldn't hear the student and asked him to repeat. You should anticipate their responses because repeating things is embarrassing for them."

"The ceiling heat vent is really loud and distracting."

"One of the lights in the back of the room is out."

"Your room wasn't decorated enough." (They had switched the teacher into that room the same day as the observation.)

"Only 19 of 22 students were engaged."

"You sound like the teacher from Ferris Bueller."

"The chalk squeaks too much when you write on the chalkboard."

"Playdough must be in individual containers, not in a bag!"

"You have too many charts hanging up." (The charts were mandated by administration.)

"When students were asked why they were reading they couldn't give a purpose other than liking reading."

"You use too many exclamation points on your board, which could seem like you are yelling at the students."

"You need to have more charisma. I can't tell you how though, you just have to figure it out."

"You need to have more small group activities." (There were only 6 kids in the class.)

"You didn't know all your students' names yet." (It was the FIRST day of school.)

"You did not have the student hand out his own papers and materials." (The student was a special education student who *literally* had no hands or feet.)

"Your lesson did not have closure." (Admin. left early and missed it.)

"The students don't talk to each other." (Students are non-verbal special education students.)

"Your laminated charts are causing a glare."

"Your co-teacher spoke during a lesson." (Are they not allowed to speak?)

"Your room smells funny." (It was a very old classroom, and all the pipes leaked, so everything smelled like mold and mildew.)

"The students are comfortable in your class; please make a better learning environment. You are not here to be liked."

"You didn't 'wow' me."

"You should have your seventh graders sit on the rug while you sit and read to them. Like circle time when I taught Pre K."

"You have too high a tolerance for misbehavior."

"The TV in the classroom next door is too loud."

"You need to change the way you point to the words on the board."

"Your lesson was not racially relevant." (It was a college level chemistry class.)

"I see a child eating pretzels out of the bag rather than on a paper towel during snack time. Please discuss proper snack techniques with your class."

"You would engage the class more if you lectured standing up." (It was a few days post knee surgery, and the teacher's crutches were against the wall behind her.)

"You have a picture up of all your students except your new student. You should have a picture up of your new student." (The new student started the day before.)

During a lesson in Spanish on the imperfect, a student raised his hand and said he didn't remember how to tell time in Spanish. The teacher told him they would have to come back to that. On her evaluation, she was marked down for "not taking advantage of a spontaneous teaching moment."

Kindergarten teacher was told, "You need to work on your singing voice. Maybe seek out a voice coach."

"You look more professional in neutral colors."

"You were too much of a teacher!"

"Try adding engagement by wearing fun jewelry."

"You sit too much." (Teacher had been in a car accident that required multiple hip procedures and recovery on crutches.)

"The toilet in your room flushes too loudly."

"You turned the lights on too fast."

"Your voice is too calm."

"You can't sing songs for fun." (She was an elementary music teacher.)

The following are real reasons that teachers were "written up:"

"After working for the district for eight years and never missing a day, I got dinged for missing too many days that year. I was taking my daughter to chemo treatments."

"Not having an ID badge even though I was never given one."

"Telling a kid to leave my classroom after she cursed me out."

"Wearing a sleeveless top in my classroom when the air conditioning was broken. It was already 90 degrees at 6:30 AM."

"Letting second graders run through the sprinkler on the beach themed week. One of the 'larger boys' got excited and took his shirt off. Admin. said it was 'just so much skin.' "

"Missing a staff meeting even though I informed them that I had a medical emergency."

"Having my ID on backward."

"I listened to a student vent about her obnoxious brothers and agreed that having younger brothers is tough. Her mother called my principal and was upset that I would agree with her daughter, so my principal wrote me up."

"I got written up for taking my kinder class to lunch five minutes early. It was the beginning of the year when I was showing them how to get to the cafeteria."

"I wrote a note home to a parent on non-school sanctioned stationery."

"I had a bottle of Febreeze behind my desk. Another teacher was in my classroom teaching, and a student walked behind my took the spray and sprayed a sleeping kid in the face. I got in trouble for having Febreeze where kids could reach it."

"I was written up for having my purse on top of the filing cabinet."

"Taking a personal day on a workshop day where our agenda included Zumba and smoothie making."

"I was written up for wearing sneakers."

"For driving my overheating car into the parking lot through the exit. The damn car was pouring smoke and nearly burst into flames, but they were concerned that I entered through the exit."

"I had a note put in my file for listening to a fellow teacher complain about the principal and not reporting what they said. Apparently, we can't have friends."

"I told a vice principal that I was pissed off about a student's behavior. He wrote me up for swearing."

"I was told by a principal that I was out of dress code for wearing leggings (with a button down shirt that was long and almost reaches my knees. I was 9 months pregnant, and they were maternity pants."

"I was written up for not giving a student a pencil. The student broke EVERY pencil he was given then refused to complete work because the pencil was broken."

"I was sitting angry."

"After a child claimed to have a gun, I searched his backpack and then I was reprimanded for 'violating a student's privacy.'"

"Was written up for watching a non-educational film with my elementary class. It was A Charlie Brown Thanksgiving, during the last period, the day before Thanksgiving."

"Throwing a piece of paper into a trash can."

"My shirt sleeves were not long enough."

"Some of my high school kids got in a car accident that I witnessed on my way into the school. Unfortunately, I saw it all happen. Thankfully, none of my kids were seriously hurt. I pulled over on the scene and waited for the cops and their parents to arrive before heading to school. I called my principal as soon as I pulled over to alert him as to why I was going to be late to school. (First period was my off period too.) I had to fill out a tardy form and sign it. It is still in my permanent file."

"Telling a kid you can't be listed as a junior with only four credits because the district handbook said you needed 12 credits. That upset the kid, and he told the principal. I was written up for 'lying to a child and causing them undo stress in their home environment. The principal listed him as a junior for his mental health even though he only had 4 credits."

"Speaking with a 5th-grade child in the hallway alone with my co-teacher and no other students about how his behavior was unacceptable after he spent the entire lunch period hitting kids on the head with a hard covered book and sent two of them to the nurse. Apparently, this embarrassed him, and his mother complained. He was moved to a different class. This was with eight days left in the school year."

"Appearing to stand aggressively near a student. I was actually trying to calm him down because he peed his pants."

"I was three minutes late for a faculty meeting. I was also pregnant and had to pee.' "

"Carrying a coffee cup in the classroom and not being 'hands-free.' "

"I was written up for taking a personal day to take my teaching certification exam. I requested the day weeks before."

"I exited the building four minutes prior to my contractual obligation."

"I had the wrong date written on the board in my classroom. Admin. said it showed how unprepared I was."

"My students were having too much fun."

"I took a day off for my own wedding."

"I was written up for having a fundraiser for things I needed in the classroom. The principal said it looked bad for the school and made it appear as though they couldn't provide everything that was needed. *But they couldn't.*"

"I got in a disagreement with a stranger online over a news article. I said I would slap them (although I had no idea who they were.) The person reversed searched my image, found out who I was and where I worked, and emailed the principal, and I got a letter in my file."

"I wore a sleeveless turtleneck on a field trip. The bus driver called the principal and said I was dressed inappropriately and I got written up."

"I allowed students to call me by my last name without the

'Ms.' part."

"I said I was going to punch the computer in the face."

"I had a sandwich on my desk. Apparently, it was 'belittling to the student in class who cannot afford a sandwich.' I was advised never to eat at work."

"I used my prep period to prepare materials for the day. I was told everything should be ready two weeks in advance."

"I said I was uncomfortable and questioned the professionalism of a teacher I was forced to co-teach with. He came in late every day and tell me of his cocaine use and drinking binges and sit in the back of the class and text. It was put in my file that I couldn't get along with a staff member. He was arrested for inappropriate conduct with a student the same year, but the letter is still in my file."

"I had three toes showing and I was written up because peep-toe apparently means only two toes can be showing."

"I was written up and given a bad evaluation score for attendance when I was out the 5 allotted days for bereavement when my dad passed away. I had to prove my father's death with a doctor's note and a copy of his death certificate."

"I told a parent in the teacher parking lot that this was not the drop off area. She said, 'Too bad' and tried to zoom out, only she smashed into a car. I walked back and took a picture of her license plate because she wasn't about to stop and leave a note. She contacted the district and said I was bullying her, and I made her hit the car. My principal called me in and told me they had to put it in my file."

"I was written up for not emailing my assistant principal about missing a class to attend a mandatory training with a different assistant principal."

"I put on my Facebook page to pray for a coworker who had just had a stroke. Admin. said it was inappropriate even though it was a private page and I didn't say the coworker's name."

"I was written up for having too much *toe cleavage!*"

"A boy randomly punched another boy in my art class. I was busy helping several students with an intricate part of their project at the time, yet I still got written up because I 'didn't have control of my classroom.'"

"I was written up for having dyed my hair a color that was not my natural color."

"For running a relaxation and yoga class after school. One of the parents thought I was trying to convert her kid to Hinduism, so I got written up."

"I said 'crap' once."

"A student reported that I was teaching witchcraft in my classroom. It was Latin. I got written up for teaching Latin."

"I got a letter in my file for standing on a filing cabinet while trying to hang up the posters the principal required us to hang up."

"I helped a group of students work through a disagreement that was leading to a fight. My class had to wait 4 minutes, so I got written up."

"I got written up for informing a parent that their son was threatening suicide. They said I did not follow procedure. I was supposed to tell the counselor first.

"I got written up for putting kids in the hall. They were making up work. A teacher walked by and ratted me out. The teacher that ratted me out slapped a kid in the hallway a few months later, and it was caught on camera. The parent even went to the police, but it was never investigated by the administration, and the teacher got no repercussions whatsoever."

"A kid started cursing in class, then escalated to throwing his shoes up at the ceiling, and it almost hit another student. He continued to be violent, and I started to worry he would hurt someone. I had called the office almost a dozen times, and despite being across the hall, no one came. I tried to remove the student but he wouldn't leave so I took my class into the hallway. My principal told me that it was unacceptable to have them there, regardless of the circumstance. The student was not given a punishment. A month later, the same student started defecating and smearing it on the walls. The first place he did it? The principal's office. *Poetic justice indeed.*"

"I was written up for not *volunteering* during the summer to write curriculum."

"I was written up for having a blind spot in my room due to a partition that the principal refuses to remove."

"I got a letter in my file for taking one day off each month to take my husband to the Veteran's Hospital for treatment. The principal said my excessive absences were going to affect the children's ability to learn, even though I told her about it during my interview before she hired me."

"I wanted to paint a motivational mural in the hallway. The school bought the red and blue paint for the background, but not the white for the lettering/border work. The school had maintenance paint the red and blue on the walls for the background boxes. I waited to paint the rest until we got the white paint I requested. I was called in and reprimanded for inciting gang violence for leaving red and blue paint up in the hallway. It's a suburban district with no gang activity.

FAQ WITH TEACHER MISERY

"It turns out, common core testing prepares our students for what they'll face as adults: pointless stress and confusion."

-Stephen Colbert

What has been your worst and best experience with an administrator?

If you read my first book *Teacher Misery,* then you know all about my worst experiences with an administrator I lovingly refer to as the Ass Principal. She was a much older woman who was condescending and gave horrible advice. She reprimanded me for calling 911 when a student was overdosing on drugs (because according to her, that decision is best left to the nurse), she responded to several of my behavioral referrals with, "Well, you're a new/young teacher so…" and then did nothing, let a kid get away with plagiarizing his entire paper but yelled at me for letting the kid write about marijuana (the same kid who sold weed in my class and did not get in trouble), and she specifically told me to "treat kids like sacks of shit." Looking back, she had been a teacher and an administrator for over 40 years, so she was probably just losing her mind. Someone needed to make her retire.

The best administrator I had was another assistant principal who would always "tell it like it is" and kept it real. She would agree with my complaints, tell me why she legitimately could not help me in certain situations and treated me with a general feeling of respect. She was no-nonsense, funny, and wasn't afraid to call a kid an asshole as soon as he left the room. I appreciate that. I should also give a shout out to my former department chair who showed she trusted me by not questioning what I was doing or why. I didn't appreciate her taking a backseat approach to leading us until I got a new chair who was up our asses, had to see and comment on everything, and was way too *into* the curriculum and standards. My former chairperson would also always back us up and advocate for us with parents and other admin., no matter the circumstance. She really "had our backs." The new one was more interested in getting on the good side of the higher-ups than building loyalty and relationships with us. He gave people reasons to complain behind his back and eventually file formal complaints, which did not work out well for him in the end. Life lesson: show respect for those who truly deserve it, not for people you think might do something for you in return.

What's the best/worst experience you've had during an observation?

The worst observations I've had include the time I didn't know I had a gigantic tomato sauce stain on my shirt and when an administrator walked in while I was setting students up for a review game. I asked them to pick team names (which I no longer do- they are automatically the Puppies and Kittens whether they like it or not) and one team chose to call themselves "The Big Dicks." I yelled at them that that was very inappropriate. One student responded, "What's inappropriate?" (I walked right into this one.) "The big dicks!" I yelled, at the exact moment that the assistant principal walked in.

The best observation I had was sheer luck. An administrator came in for a surprise observation on a day when I had planned one of the best lessons I have ever made. I spent years perfecting this particular lesson. It had everything any administrator or curriculum writer could ask for, met every standard, and was actually extremely engaging. Plus, I had taught it so many times I really knew what I was talking about and could anticipate any issues that might arise during the lesson. That class also had few kids with behavioral problems to begin with, so none of that came up. The administrator was so impressed that she told everyone how wonderful my teaching is, which was nice. She even skipped observing me for a few years *(yes, years),* because she felt that what she saw that day was enough to ensure several years' worth of confidence. That probably wasn't the best idea, but hey, I had no problem with it! If she had seen any other class that week, it would have unfolded quite differently.

How can we elevate the field back to being a career path that is respected?

The only thing I can think of is to try to give the general public a window into what teaching is really like. School is so different than it ever was because of social media and technology, and people need to understand how difficult that makes our job. Sharing our experiences is so important. That is why I started writing about what was occurring when I first started teaching. I was unaware of how difficult it was, and I *needed* people to know!

How do you find the time to manage Teacher Misery and publish books etc. while teaching?

I wrote most of my first book during the summer before I had kids of my own. I was lucky enough not to need to work that summer (call it luck or stupidity because I drained my savings account). Writing about what goes on at school is not only a pleasurable hobby for me, it is therapy. Sometimes my experiences are like poison, and I have to stop everything to extract it. I try to steal small moments to jot down a story or my feelings whenever I can. If I didn't have this outlet, I would not be able to keep teaching. I was in therapy for a long time at the beginning of my career. My therapist revealed that more than half of her huge practice (which included several other therapists and psychiatrists) were teachers. She started a support group for teachers too. When I stopped going to her, I started writing and posting online. It is very important to have an outlet, or the negativity will eat away at your soul. *Teacher Misery* might be super negative, but that is where I put the bad stuff. There are other aspects of my life that aren't miserable (I think), but obviously, I don't need to expel that stuff. The shit that goes on at work *needs* to be shared. Before I found my outlet, I would end up in some very awkward situations at dinner parties and such. Someone would ask the innocent question, "How's teaching?" and I would launch into a crazy tirade that lasted an awkwardly long amount of time. Now that I have my outlet I no longer have to preach. I just say, "Read my book."

Assuming that teaching was your first career choice, what was your second choice?

I kind of always knew I would be a teacher. I was the class clown growing up, but not in a disruptive way (*I don't think*). I got good grades, but I was so bored that I had to make everything a joke. My favorite classes were always English and theater even though English class was still quite boring. I just knew I could make it better. I saw the classroom as my own audience, where I could crack jokes, have deep discussions and make literature fun. When I first started college, I tried to fight the call to teach. I was vaguely aware of how challenging it would be, and I had just gotten out of high school. I wasn't thrilled about going back for another 30 years. So I majored in sociology with the intention of becoming a therapist. So much of the teaching job is acting as a therapist for kids who have no one to talk to. This is one of the hardest parts of the job, but also the most rewarding. It is particularly challenging as a teacher because after teaching five classes you don't have much time or energy left to act as a personal therapist. Sometimes I think I should have just been a school counselor or school psychologist, but when I see how much paperwork they have, I know that it isn't any easier than what I do every day.

When I first started studying sociology and psychology in college, it was mandatory that we volunteer a certain amount of hours at the campus crisis center. It was a walk-in center and hotline for anyone in distress. I volunteered for two years, and it was the unhealthiest thing I could have done for myself. I have battled severe depression since I was a teenager and the scenarios presented at the crisis center did not help my state of mind. The training process was extremely intensive (perhaps too intensive). I spent most of the two years doing role-play exercises. Other volunteers would pretend to be a person in crisis, and I would practice how to help them. I cried a lot. It put me in a very dark place, but I was determined to pass the training and become an official peer counselor. The final test was given at a retreat. The group rented a number of cabins in a wooded, desolate location. For three days we played a number of games, talked a lot and really bonded. I knew there was some kind of clandestine ritual that I would have to pass through on the last night. It was a big secret, and now I understand why. If I knew what I was about to go through I would never have signed up in the first place.

In the middle of the night, we were woken up and told to meet in a certain location. When we arrived, it was explained that to be a good therapist one must be ready to handle anything, even the most extreme scenarios. This ritual would test our ability to handle a series of crises. We were each given a different number and told to enter the cabin with the corresponding number. When we entered the cabin, there was some kind of horrific situation going on that we had to deal with. The first was an actor walking around with a machete and babbling about how he was going to kill everyone. I tried to talk him out of it, and five minutes later they blew a whistle, and I had to leave that cabin and enter the next sequential cabin. The next cabin had a girl ready to commit suicide; then there was a girl who was pregnant and didn't know what to do, next there was someone who had murdered a friend and needed someone to talk to, then I was alone in a cabin in the dark when the phone rang. I answered it, and it was a person talking about committing suicide and then promptly hanging up. When I finally got to the last cabin, there was a man lying in bed holding a bible. I kept trying to get him to talk, and he was eerily silent until he finally spoke, "I have terminal cancer. I am going to die." At that point, I dropped to my knees and cried my eyes out. I lost a parent to cancer when I was a child. I couldn't take anymore. The actor immediately dropped his character and joined me on the floor. He apologized over and over and revealed that he thought the whole ritual they were engaged in was insane. Afterward, we convened to "debrief." They all heard about my breakdown and were very supportive. I passed the test and was declared an official peer counselor. But I knew that whole deal was just not for me and I never actually counseled a real peer. Obviously, that whole scenario was ridiculous, but I didn't really want to deal with *any* of the situations I was presented with. I knew it was very unhealthy for me. Ironically, I deal with those scenarios with my students every now and again. But not exactly one after another, there are usually a few days in between. (I probably didn't need to share all of that, but it was interesting to read about, *wasn't it?*)

For a while, I had the idea to officiate weddings. I even got ordained at the Universal Life Church (which merely involves filling out a form on their webpage.) I thought, "Okay, I'm a good public speaker, and I'm funny. I know a lot of love poetry, both Christian and Jewish customs, and I am happily married. Officiants in my region make $300-$1,000 for 30 minutes' worth of work. Why can't I do this?" I made a webpage and started to research how to list myself on wedding websites, and then it got really complicated and expensive, and I realized that I would be giving up my weekends (if I even got enough business). It never went anywhere, but I didn't really try that hard. As I'm explaining it now, I think it still might not be a bad idea. Does anybody need a minister? Email me at TeacherMisery1@gmail.com!

How are you able to tell it like it is without getting in trouble? Most districts frown on our doing this.

I wrote these books and run my social media accounts under a pen name. Unfortunately, I cannot tell anyone at work about my books. I worked hard to make sure that there are no details in my writing that are clues to where I teach. I had other people look for the same things just to make sure. At the end of the day, if I was "found out," I really don't think there would be repercussions because the book does not name names, and it's a matter of free speech/press. I'd love for this to be a public fight I could take to the media. "My district fired me for telling the world how they treated me!"

From your posts, I assume you're a parent, too. How do you balance parenthood with teaching?

I'm going to be honest with you. I do not do nearly as much as many other teachers. If I did, there is no way I would survive as both a teacher and a mom. A lot of the time I just can't believe that I became the "behavior correction lady." All day long I correct poor teenage behavior, and at all other times, I am correcting irrational toddler behavior. It doesn't come naturally to me. I have a hard time following through and not laughing. My kids are more important than anyone else's kids, and I must prioritize. I do the best I can at work, but as they say, I LEAVE WORK AT WORK (except for venting on social media). In a lot of ways, I think teaching makes us better parents. We know what different kinds of kids are like and how to handle them. It also makes us worry more, I'm sure. My kids are in preschool, and I am already worrying about social media and their mental health. But being with teens all day makes me appreciate sitting and coloring with my kids or watching *My Little Pony*.

What subjects, activities, lessons, etc. would you like to incorporate into your teaching if you didn't have to spend so much time on standardized testing?

Anything that involves critical thinking! My favorite thing to do is give them very open-ended journal topics to make them have to think a little bit. The prompt will often be merely one word such as "love." It's interesting how many kids freak out over this kind of assignment. They are used to spitting back what they've been told in a certain format. All I ask them to do is fill a page with thoughts, in any format they choose. They ask a million questions. Many just sit there stumped. I tell them not to worry about what they are writing, just to write.

They still don't know what to write. It takes some of them an entire semester to get comfortable writing without being told what to write. A lot of them get angry or act irritated, but at the end of every school year, it is the single thing that kids consistently say was their favorite. Unfortunately, there is less and less time to do things like this because someone is always mandating what we are doing. I am going to make a set day and time when we always do these journals, no matter what, so we make it a priority. I know they get a lot more out of it than preparing to take a test that asks them to analyze figurative language.

Do you really dread the work as much as you make it seem - or do you secretly love it?

I know that deep down I love it because after a few weeks of summer I really do miss it. I still get excited when I see a funny magnet to put on my whiteboard or a cool jar that would make a great "cell phone prison." I still enjoy decorating my room before every school year. There is still hope every September that the next crop of kids will be better. Not all of it has been beaten out of me yet.

Why has our society allowed teachers and the teaching profession to become so underappreciated? If it wasn't for their first-grade teacher teaching them to read where would they be? If it wasn't for that one HS teacher, who inspired them to go further? What about us? Where are our credit and respect? Why do people hate teachers?

I've thought about this a lot. I think the main issue is that everybody went to school, so everybody thinks they know what it's like to be a teacher because they were a student. They have no idea what it's like on the other side of the desk. I thought I knew what a teacher's job was like when I was in high school. The reason I wanted to be a teacher was I *knew* I could do a better job. And some of that was true because my English teachers had zero passion and never bothered to make anything interesting. I thought, "I can read this with a lot more passion and make it fun," but I had no idea about all the other things that these people were dealing with. I was judging their experience based on the one class I had with them. I never considered that they teach the same thing five or six times a day and that the curriculum might seriously limit how much creativity they can bring to the lesson, not to mention how exhausted they probably were from dealing with kids all day and going home to their own families.

I also think that a lot of people see teaching as something they could do if they wanted to like it's something anybody could do. You will hear that saying… those who can *do* and those who can't, *teach*. I don't know how many times I've heard that and wanted to smack somebody. In fact, when I have students challenge me that they could do a better job teaching or could control the class better, I call their bluff. I say, "Okay, tomorrow you're teaching a lesson on X or on whatever you want." They almost always start with excitement, get flustered and embarrassed, and eventually concede that it is much harder than they had once thought.

The other aspect is the notion that we knew what the job would be like before we signed up, so we shouldn't complain. Everyone knows teachers get paid shit and are often treated like shit, so what did we expect? If this were the case, there would be no teachers! Just because it has always been this way does not make it okay. Plus, it has gotten exponentially harder over the last decade. I became a teacher based on what I experienced in the classroom in the late nineties. If I knew about social media and what classrooms would be like today, would have tried very hard to find something else that would fulfill me. (In the end, I'd probably still teach because *if we don't do it, who will?*)

What do you do for self-care?

I sleep and hang out with my dogs as much as possible. I also pay for after school care for my own kids so I can decompress for a bit before I have to pick them up. It is worth every penny. To be able to sit on the couch with my dogs in a quiet house, staring at piles of laundry and a sink full of dirty dishes, means the world to me. My husband doesn't have that, and I don't know how he goes right from a stressful work day into kids jumping all over him and whining about bath time and surprise eggs. Then again, he doesn't spend the entire day with angst-ridden teenagers.

What do you do if you get an angry email from a parent who just won't accept her child's grade (because the little darling chose not to contribute to the group project)?

I give as full of an explanation I can, with all kinds of stupid documentation, rubrics, and examples. If they don't go away after that, I forward that shit to my chairperson, and they usually take it from there. Sometimes their grade gets changed, but if I let that bother me, I'd have had a bleeding ulcer many years ago.

What do you think is the best part about being a teacher (besides summer)? In other words, what keeps you going?

What keeps me going despite the miserable conditions are the lessons I handcrafted that I still get really excited about. Also, the students who comment to their friend "I like this class" or "this class is gonna be good" on their way out of my first class of the year. The kids who say that it turns out that Shakespeare isn't that hard to understand and is actually interesting, give me life. The students who tell me, "I never liked English class or reading until I had you. Now I love it!" mean everything to me. It's the best feeling in the world, and the reason I became a teacher. I never forget kids who are like a block of ice at the beginning of the year but become some of my favorite students. I keep going for the kids who desperately need someone to encourage them; the ones who come back years later to tell me the impact I had on their life. The best part is the particularly small percentage of students who are grateful to be there, try their hardest to improve, and are just mature, thoughtful, amazing human beings. I learn from them, and they change *my* life too.

Every year, no matter how bad the overall behavior and attitude of my classes, there are a handful of students that I get to know really well. They are the ones I will remember forever. Sometimes it's a kid I pulled under my wing because I could tell he was taking drugs and I got him help, or a girl who was way too hard on herself and needed pep talks to be kinder to herself, or the boy who lost a parent and needed someone to talk to. At the end of every year, graduation feels very profound for me, not because of the greatness of education (many of these kids didn't pass anything and really shouldn't be graduating), but because of the connections, I have made with so many students. I have specific memories for each student who crosses the stage, and though many of them are not necessarily heartwarming memories, there is always a bit of personal growth or a softening of a kid's attitude to think of. I am always shocked when a kid who gave me a terrible attitude all year is so excited to see me in the hallway the following year. Kids mostly just need someone to talk to, someone to treat them kindly-- even if they are being a douche (and BOY is that challenging), and someone who is willing to listen to their story. It's too much to ask, because *we have to actually teach them things as well,* but it is so important. I know for some kids I am one of the only positive adults in their life. Even if it isn't obvious, I know that some kids will remember my humor and kindness and perhaps try to live in a similar way. Yes, friends, it's true. Even Teacher Misery has a heart.

"Life goes by fast. Enjoy it.

Calm down. It's all funny."

-Joan Rivers

Hold on, lemme finish up here and I'll be right with you.

Natalie Dee.com

ABOUT THE AUTHOR

Jane Morris is the pen name of a teacher who would really like to tell you more about herself, but she is afraid she'll lose her job. She has taught English for over 12 years in a major American city. She received her B.A. in English and Secondary Education from a well-known university. She earned her M.A. in Writing from an even fancier (more expensive) university. She loves dogs and trees and other things that can't talk. She has a loving family and cares about making people laugh more than anything else. Visit TeacherMisery.com for a place to anonymously vent about your teaching experiences. You can also follow *Teacher Misery* on Instagram, Twitter, Facebook, and Tumblr and if you are into that sort of thing. Otherwise, just move on with your life.

SOURCES

[1] From about 1985 to 1995, Keds canvas sneakers were very popular with pubescent girls and their moms. They were often worn with slouch socks pulled over leggings.

[2] Chokshi, Niraj. "Yes, People Really Are Eating Tide Pods. No, It's Not Safe." *The New York Times*, 20 Jan. 2018.

[3] *Ibid.*

[4] Hassan, Jennifer. "Arrests, Fines and Injuries: The 'In My Feelings' Challenge Has Gone Global, with Dangerous Results." *The Washington Post*, WP Company, 31 July 2018.

[5] The Individualized Education Program, also called the **IEP**, is a document that is developed for each public school child who needs special education.

[6] Toppo, Greg. "What You Need to Know about Betsy DeVos." *USA Today*, Gannett Satellite Information Network, 7 Feb. 2017.

[7] Strauss, Valerie. "Analysis | Like It or Not, Betsy DeVos Has Made a Mark in Six Months as Education Secretary." *The Washington Post*, WP Company, 4 Aug. 2017.

[8] Stanton, Zack. How Betsy Devos Used God and Amway to Take Over Michigan Politics. *Politico*. January, 15, 2017.

[9] Biblical location where David and Goliath were said to have fought

[10] Stanton, Zack. How Betsy Devos Used God and Amway to Take Over Michigan Politics. Politico. January, 15, 2017.

[11] *Ibid.*

[12] Yeah, we're on a first name basis.

[13] Stanton, Zack. How Betsy Devos Used God and Amway to Take Over Michigan Politics. Politico. January, 15, 2017.

[14] *Ibid.*

[15] Bottari, Mary. "Betsy DeVos Ethics Report Reveals Ties to Student Debt Collection Firm." *PR Watch*, 27 Jan. 2017.

[16] *Ibid.*

[17] Kelly, Kate. "School Vouchers: What You Need to Know." *Understood.org*, 2018.

[18] Prothero, Arianna. "'There Is No Oversight': Private-School Vouchers Can Leave Parents on Their Own." *Education Week*, Editorial Project in Education, 20 June 2018.

[19] "10 Reasons Why Private School Vouchers Should Be Rejected." *Americans United for Separation of Church and State*, Feb. 2011.

[20] Balingit, Moriah, and Danielle Douglas-Gabriel. "Congress Rejects Much of Betsy DeVos's Agenda in Spending Bill." *The Washington Post*, WP Company, 24 Mar. 2018.

[21] Jamieson, Alistair. "Betsy DeVos Cites Grizzly Bears during Guns-in-Schools Debate." *NBCNews.com*, NBCUniversal News Group, 17 Jan. 2017.

[22] Bottari, Mary. "Betsy DeVos Ethics Report Reveals Ties to Student Debt Collection Firm." *PR Watch*, 27 Jan. 2017.

[23] "Betsy DeVos." *Betsy DeVos - SourceWatch*, www.sourcewatch.org/index.php/Betsy_DeVos.

[24] *Ibid.*

[25] "DeVos picks private student loan chief to head government loan program," The Washington Post, June 21, 2017.

[26] Mulhere, Kaitlin. "Education Department Voids Rule Barring Collection Fees | Money." *Time*, 17 Mar. 2017.

[27] Strauss, Valerie. "Analysis- Like It or Not, Betsy DeVos Has Made a Mark in Six Months as Education Secretary." *The Washington Post*, WP Company, 4 Aug. 2017.

[28] Karlis, Nicole. "Betsy DeVos Halts Debt Relief for Defrauded Students." *Salon*, 13 Dec. 2017,

[29] Saha, Ria. "85 Illegal Or Banned Baby Names From Around The World." *MomJunction*, Incnut, 9 July 2018.

[30] Gillett, Rachel. "60 Banned Baby Names from around the World." *Business Insider*, Business Insider, 8 Nov. 2017.

[31] Staff, Credible. "How Teachers Can Save Thousands On Their Student Loans." *Credible*, 9 Feb. 2018,

[32] "Jobs Home- City of New York." *Zoning Districts & Tools : C6 - DCP*,

www1.nyc.gov/jobs/index.page.

[33] "50 High-Paying Jobs That Don't Require a College Degree." *Nwitimes.com*, 20 Oct. 2017.

[34] Bennett, Troy. "Paying Enough and Training Right! A Snapshot of Salary, Benefits, and Professional Development Practices in Camps." *American Camp Association*, 10 Aug. 2016.

[35] A popular meme from 2012.

[36] Warzel, Charlie. "2/26: The Oral History". *BuzzFeed*, February 2018.

[37] *Ibid.*

[38] "The blue and black (or white and gold) dress: Actual colour, brand, and price details revealed." *The Independent*. 27 February 2015.

[39] "Sign the Petition." *Change.org*, www.change.org/p/cincinnati-zoo-justice-for-harambe.

[40] Criss, Doug. "No, Harambe Didn't Get 11,000 Votes for President." *CNN*, Cable News Network, 10 Nov. 2016.

[41] Covucci, David. "Auction for Hot Cheetos Harambe Goes Viral on EBay." The Daily Dot, 7 Mar. 2017.

[42] Weller, Chris. "There's an Epidemic of Grade Inflation and Unearned As in American High Schools." *Business Insider*, Business Insider, 18 July 2017.

[43] *Study.com*, Study.com, study.com/academy/lesson/mixed-ability-grouping-advantages-disadvantages.html.

[44] *Ibid.*

[45] Fagles, Robert. *The Odyssey*. Penguin Classics; Reprint edition November 29, 1999.

[46] Hinds, Gareth. *The Odyssey*. Candlewick; First Edition (US) First Printing edition October 12, 2010.

[47] https://jprc.wested.org/wp-content/uploads/2016/02/RJ_Literature-Review_20160217.pdf

[48] Sperry, Paul. "How Liberal Discipline Policies Are Making Schools Less Safe." *New York Post*, New York Post, 15 Mar. 2015.

[49] *Ibid.*

[50] "Discipline Concerns Flare in Denver Schools." *Chalkbeat*, 14 May 2013.

[51] Riley, Jason. "An Obama Decree Continues to Make Public Schools Lawless." *The Wall Street Journal*, 21 Mar. 2017.

[52] Sperry, Paul. "How Liberal Discipline Policies Are Making Schools Less Safe." *New York Post*, New York Post, 15 Mar. 2015.

[53] Brodsky, Sascha. "Is Discipline Reform Really Helping Decrease School Violence?" *The Atlantic*, Atlantic Media Company, 28 June 2016.

[54] Perez, Juan. "Teachers Complain about Revised CPS Discipline Policy." *Chicagotribune.com*, 25 Feb. 2015.

"Syracuse Teachers' Union: 'Restorative Justice' Is Fine, but What about Immediate Safety?" *Syracuse.com*, 8 Apr. 2014.

[56] Walsh, James. "St. Paul Teachers Threaten Strike over School Violence." *Star Tribune*, Star Tribune, 10 Dec. 2015.

[57] Watanabe, Teresa, and Howard Blume. "Why Some LAUSD Teachers Are Balking at a New Approach to Discipline Problems." *Los Angeles Times*, Los Angeles Times, 7 Nov. 2015.

[58] *Ibid.*

[59] *Ibid.*

[60] Huber, Dave. "'Liberal Discipline Policies' Are Making Schools Dangerous." *The College Fix*, 18 Mar. 2015.

Sperry, Paul. "How Liberal Discipline Policies Are Making Schools Less Safe." *New York Post*, New York Post, 15 Mar. 2015.

[62] Palmer, Tyrone. "The Booty-Eating Renaissance." *Gawker*, gawker.com/the-booty-eating-renaissance-1633706123.

[63] Cuz I'm not that hip.

[64] Galerie, Nue. "Warning: A Column on Butt Stuff." *The Cut*, 8 Apr. 2014.

[65] Cartwright, Dana. "You're Doing It Wrong: Tossing Salad- You've Got Gas." *Complex*, 20 Dec. 2017.

[66] Skeet is a slang term for ejaculation.

Made in the USA
San Bernardino, CA
01 April 2019